"Janville"

A STORY OF GRACE AND REDEMPTION

"GETTING RID OF MYSELF TO FIND MYSELF"

Jan and Greg Naylor

CrossLink Publishing
RAPID CITY, SD

Naylor/CrossLink Publishing
1601 Mt Rushmore Rd. Ste 3288
Rapid City, SD 57701
www.CrossLinkPublishing.com

Ordering Information:
Quantity sales. Special discounts are available on quantity purchases by corporations, associations, and others. For details, contact the "Special Sales Department" at the address above.

Janville/Jan and Greg Naylor. —1st ed.
ISBN 978-1-63357-372-7
Library of Congress Control Number: 2020950660

"The Confession" by Beth Moore, reprinted and used by permission.

Dedication

This book is dedicated to my children, my grandchildren, my sister, and my close friends. Along with my relationships with Jesus and my husband, my family and friends mean everything to me. Without their support and encouragement, I'm certain that my story would be one of sadness and regret rather than one of hope and optimism.

To my sons, I love each of you from the bottom of my heart. I have always tried to sacrifice for you and to provide a loving, stable home environment for you. I am so sorry that you experienced challenges and losses as result of the difficult relationship I shared with your dad. However, please know that your parents both loved you and always cared about your best interests. Please also know that I feel I have a calling from Christ to tell my story to help others. It is not told to embarrass or hurt anyone but to show how a relationship with Jesus can lift us out of chaos and despair. Perhaps the most effective testimony I can offer for Jesus is simply that of talking about my own life mistakes.

To my sis, I so appreciate your insight into people. Your strength and your sense of humor have helped keep me upright. Neither of us have had smooth sailing through the years but we have been there for each other.

To my special friends, C., S., J., Sy, Ce, and K., I have so valued our friendships and appreciated your advice. You have also lived my story with me. I'm so thankful that, partially due to your support, I now truly appreciate my joyful life after previously existing in a life filled with unhappiness, uncertainty, and disruption.

Contents

Dedication v

Preface 1

Conclusion 3

Section One: Learning How to Ruin a Life 7

    A Rolling Stone Gathers No Moss 7

    Dad's Drinking and Lectures 9

    Mom's Drinking and My Need for Control 9

    A Man's Approval 10

    Running Away from Home 11

    Arguing with an Alcoholic 12

    Talking and Laughing: My Human Connections 13

    The Ultimate People Pleaser 14

    Manipulation and Quid Pro Quo 14

    Jill and Jesus: Searching for My BFF 15

Section Two: Carrying Baggage into Adulthood 17

    Meeting Bill: Not Your Typical Guy 17

    The Hernandez Group 20

Attending Village Bible Church.. 21

Bill's Proposal and My Parents' Reaction: A "Marriage Made in
Heaven"?.. 22

Marriage, a Baby, and Attendance at VBC 23

The "Flexible" Fidelity Pledge 24

Leaving VBC and the "Crabby Christians" 26

New Members at Christian Community Church........................... 26

Leading in the Church and Leading at Home 28

Our Family Celebrations: Happy Fifth of July 28

Learning to Cope: Just Weather the Storm 32

Tearstained Letters of Loneliness.. 32

The Devil in "Pretty" Clothes?... 33

Divorce #1: Exchanging a Sin for a Sin 37

"Biblically Based" Arguments to Control and Intimidate............ 39

My Escape to John.. 41

The Annulment Cake.. 42

The Power of Guilt and Shame... 43

John: Take Two 45

The Reprise . . . Marriage #2 to Bill 46

Our Hawaii Honeymoon and Janine 46

Church as Punishment.. 48

The Call Back to Chaos... 49

Taking Bill Back . . . Again 50

Church Sex Scandal Rocks CCC 51

Filling My Spiritual Void 52

Isolation from Family and Friends 52

**Section Three: More Janplans . . . Different Facts,
Same Results** 55

An Old Friend Resurfaces 55

Frank and Divorce #2 from Bill 57

My Sixteen-Day Marriage to Frank 58

"Quid Pro Quo" Family Dysfunction 59

Marriage #3: Back on the Not-So-Merry-Go-Round 60

Choosing to Stand Up or Sit Down 61

"Vacation Bill": My Dream Husband 63

Life Compartments: My Key to Sanity 64

The Girl Who Jumped into Bill's Truck 65

Bill's Retirement: His Free Time = My Full Time 66

Chat Room Pop-Ups 67

The Girl in the Prescription Bottle 68

The Death of *PollyJana*: Hating the Person I'd Become 70

Porn Again, Not Born Again 71

Trying to Buy Happiness 72

Filling the Void with Small-g Gods 74

Searching for "Vacation Bill" One Final Time:
Our 2014 UK Trip 77

Beginning to *Janplan* My Final Exit 78

The Craziest *Janplan*: Did the Devil Make Me Do It? 80

Seeking God's Stamp of Approval 81

The Quest: Searching for Jan in All the Wrong Places 82

Jan, the International Ping-Pong Ball 83

Section Four: Rediscovering My Faith and My Family 85

Searching for a Rock—Not Another Man 85

My Epiphany: Rain, Hail, and Jesus Washed Me Clean 87

Dismantling, Releasing, and Listening 96

Children, Grandchildren, and Unconditional Love 97

Returning to Jesus on the Return Home 99

Shelter for the Body and the Soul 101

Katie and Stan: Christian Community and Service 103

Returning to Church: A "Get To" Not a "Got To" Activity 104

God's Voice in a Moment of Confusion 105

Children's Hospital: God's Healing Touch 106

God's Next Miracle: Providing My Christian Partner 107

Bill's Gone: What Is the Cost of "Freedom"? 113

My Transformed, Personal Relationship with Jesus 114

No *PollyJana*, *Janville*, or *Janplans*: Living a Real Life with Jesus.. 116

My Simple Answer Can Be Your Simple Answer 118

The Confession 119

Preface

I didn't want to write this book. It's about my wife, Jan, whom I love dearly, and it recounts her marital and faith struggles over several decades. It's not a flattering picture of her or her previous relationships.

After Jan and I met, she was honest about the emotional abuse she had suffered and about the ups and downs she had experienced in her faith journey. In between tears, she would occasionally joke that her life story was so "interesting" that several friends had encouraged her to write a book. We would both roll our eyes and quickly move to another subject. However, after Jan's counselor encouraged her to journal her feelings about some of her past experiences, I actually felt a nudge from God to help Jan write her story.

As we prayed about it, Jan and I realized that we needed to think of her story from a different perspective. After all, God often uses some of his most challenged children to reveal His stories of grace and transformation. Perhaps Christ wanted Jan to recount her earlier life of emotional abuse, codependency, and timid faith to help others struggling with similar challenges. Perhaps my past marital problems, my inconsistent walk with Jesus, and my writing experience could be used to compliment Jan's gifts and her story. Perhaps our Christian partnership was not only a prayer answered for us but also a union we could use to encourage others to turn away from their past failures and toward Jesus . . . to accept the love, grace, and redemption that He so freely offers each of us.

Special thanks also to Dom, Henry, K.C., Gene, Cynthia, Joey, John, Kara, Brandon, Nga, and Jerry for their candid insights and thoughtful advice on the book . . . this couldn't have happened without the support and prayers of our Christian brothers and sisters.

—Greg A. Naylor

Conclusion

S o who writes a conclusion and sticks it at the beginning of the book?

It made sense to me because the conclusion to my story is so simple. In fact, the solution I found for the serious emotional abuse I experienced for years might just be the answer to any problems you have as well. Here it is: *Jesus saved me.* Really.

It's that straightforward. He performed a miracle in my life. My personal relationship with Him transformed my life from one of severe emotional abuse, chaos, continual disappointment, ongoing anger, and pain to one of joy, peace, and overall contentment.

Let me take a step back now to actually tell you my story. The events in this book are all true. I lived them, reflected on them, anguished over them, and allowed them to change me, in ways both good and bad.

The names of some people and locations in my story have been changed to protect the privacy of family and friends. In many respects, however, their names really don't matter. Rather, it was their relationships with me that helped create the tapestry of my life—a cloth that Jesus knitted together, binding it all with His grace and His love, to wrap around me and to comfort me even as He provided the light to chase away the darkness that enveloped my life.

Here are a few facts that have defined much of my life journey:

- *I've been married six times. I married the same man, Bill, three times. I spent over four decades with Bill. In between my marriages to Bill, I married two other men, for a combined total of twenty-seven days, before I filed for divorce from each of them only to re-marry Bill again.*

- *Bill was an alcoholic. He had multiple affairs, was into pornography and sex chat rooms, accumulated phone numbers and email addresses from other women, failed to call or come home hundreds of times, lied repeatedly about his outside activities, helped very little around the home, spent the vast majority of his free time on his hobbies, rarely spent any time with me, and repeatedly used harsh anger, intimidation, and criticism to manipulate me and control our marriages.*

- *To cut the cord that kept me tied me to Bill, I ran away to a foreign country only to return two months later, homeless, without a job or any income, humiliated and ashamed of my decision to escape.*

I think I know a couple of the things you might be thinking. Why would anyone stay in a marriage plagued by such serious problems? Further, once out, why would anyone return to the same relationship over and over?

My answers are offered in the pages that follow . . . answers born out of a toxic mixture of emotional abuse and manipulation, substance addiction and codependent responses to it, confused religious doctrine, unrealistic romantic dreams, fear, and abundant amounts of self-pride.

Still, this really isn't a book about Bill or even about me. Rather, it's a book about the redemptive power of God's grace. It's a true story that illustrates how Christ can use His miraculous, transforming love to mold even the most twisted, ill-shaped lump of clay into something beautiful—a person capable of having a trusting, authentic relationship with Him and healthy, loving relationships with other people. Jesus still performs miracles. I am living proof that He can, and will, save a person's life.

I look forward to having you join me as I tell my story. As you read, consider whether any part of your life journey might potentially intersect, however briefly, with mine, perhaps in one of the following ways:

- *If you've been a victim of emotional or physical abuse, my story might provide a light to help lead you out of your dark tunnel of pain and humiliation.*
- *If you've spent years looking into the eyes of others seeking acceptance and approval, my story might give you the encouragement you need to learn to love and accept yourself.*
- *If you fear the uncertainty of a life alone, perhaps as a single mom, my story might show you that your fears will disappear once you grab the hand of your Creator.*
- *If you grew up in a conservative church and misinterpreted the message of Christianity to be a bunch of harsh rules, followed by judgment and condemnation, my story might point you to a loving Jesus.*
- *If you've never trusted Jesus enough to truly accept the grace He offers, my story might help you free yourself from the chains of your past.*
- *If you've been searching for something to fill an emptiness you feel in your life, my story might help point you to your God-given purpose.*

I've included several Bible verses in my book. I did so not to be preachy, but to illustrate how the Bible can provide spiritual insight and meaningful answers for our life problems. The Bible is God's "owner's manual"—it will keep our lives running smoothly, if we are willing to read it and take to heart its divine guidance.

Jesus saved me and He can save you. But He also asks for our participation. We must believe in Him, be willing to follow His teachings, and accept the love, salvation, and redemptive grace He so freely offers us.

> "If you hold to my teaching, you are really my disciples.
> Then you will know the truth and the truth will set you free."
> —John 8:31–32 NIV

"I am the way and the truth and the life. No one comes
to the Father except through me."

—John 14:6 NIV

Learning How to Ruin a Life

Of course, no one sets out to ruin their life. We all want those things in life that we think will make us happy. Sometimes, however, life circumstances, our reactions to those life events, and the expectations we have for our lives can combine to create a rocky life path—a path more likely to lead to a cliff than to a pleasant, downhill stroll.

I was fortunate to come from an upper-middle-class family. We had country clubs, swimming pools, and upscale shopping; I took piano, dance, cello, and horseback riding lessons. Money was never an issue. However, when some of my life expectations didn't match my life experiences, the misalignment produced conflict, anxiety, and poor decisions. Here's how things started . . .

A Rolling Stone Gathers No Moss

I attended nine different schools before I graduated from high school. I wasn't a military brat. Dad was an executive for a manufacturing company. His ascension up the corporate ladder had us constantly on the move as he pursued the next big promotion.

Dad was a self-made man from a poor family. He was smart and resilient. He also started drinking and smoking at age eleven. His vocational training as a welder and his sales acumen ultimately combined to award him a vice president title and a corner office in a high-rise in Los Angeles overlooking the Staples Center.

Mom also came from a poor family, but she was bright and intended to go to college. She remained angry that Dad's ultimatum of marriage or college denied her a higher education. Although she assumed the housewife role, Mom wasn't particularly good at it. Further, her occasional lack of good judgment at home and in public settings rankled Dad. In turn, Mom grew to resent Dad's career, including his frequent business trips, his regular business golf outings, and his two-martini lunches.

Their marriage taught me that a wife's job was to handle everything at home while the breadwinner pursued his career and hobbies. Despite my exposure to the women's rights movement in my teens, it never really captured me. My parents' more traditional, 1950s-style marriage provided my frame of reference for male–female relationships.

Unfortunately, their marriage also seemed essentially emotionless. While Mom was a source of some warmth for my sister Beth and me, I rarely saw a shred of real affection between my parents. Mom seemed to be an embarrassment to Dad. My father's controlling, stern manner with Mom made it seem like he was the father of three daughters, not just two.

Beth was five years younger than me. The difference in our ages made it hard for her to understand some of the dysfunctional family dynamics that ultimately shaped our personalities and our life decisions, even decades after we both left home.

I have some very early childhood memories of bedtime prayers and infrequent visits to Sunday school while we lived in Louisville, Kentucky. However, to me, Jesus was just some bearded guy in a bathrobe on a flannelgraph board. The teachers said He loved us. I wasn't sure what that even meant.

Mom and Dad weren't church attenders, though they claimed to be believers. In retrospect, I understand now that Beth and I never experienced the type of Christian upbringing and church community that can help kids understand that Jesus really is God, our Savior and

Redeemer—someone we can turn to for comfort and support in the bad times, someone we should praise in the good times, and someone to joyously thank for our blessings at all times.

Dad's Drinking and Lectures

Dad was a "controlled" alcoholic. Controlled in the sense that he never acknowledged he had a drinking problem because his drinking didn't prevent him from performing at work or in a social setting.

After the second or third drink, Dad's stern lectures at the dinner table would start. He would instruct Mom about how to handle things on the home front while simultaneously reminding Beth and me to keep our elbows off the table, our napkins on our laps, and our mouths shut when chewing.

To Dad, manners and lessons learned outside of school were far more important than grades and education provided in the classroom. He drummed it into Beth and me that a person is never given a second chance to make a first impression. Dinners at the country club often elicited compliments from fellow diners on the good manners exhibited by the cute Wilson girls.

Clothing also mattered to Dad. He wanted his wife and his daughters to look good in public. He frequently countermanded Mom on her clothing choices. He also instructed her to take his girls to upscale clothing stores, not Sears and J. C. Penney, the stores Mom preferred.

In contrast, Mom never outgrew her impoverished childhood. Every dollar mattered to her right up to the day she passed away. In fact, in her later years, she was much better at reciting the value of her property and stock holdings than she was at reciting the names of her grandchildren.

Mom's Drinking and My Need for Control

In my early childhood years, Mom didn't drink. However, because Dad's drinking made him much more argumentative, I always believed Mom started drinking as survival technique. She apparently decided she had to fight fire with fire.

Mom's drink of choice was beer. Unfortunately, she didn't handle alcohol well. After a couple of drinks, her stumbling and slurred speech quickly revealed her foolish side. "UTI" (under the influence) Mom embarrassed me several times in front of my friends before I graduated from high school.

Interesting how the mental picture of soused Dad and Mom, seared in my brain, was enough to keep me from ever using alcohol or recreational drugs to excess. Unfortunately, as Beth and I grew up, my parents' escalating bouts with the bottle would almost inevitably lead to arguments. Many of their battles were very heated . . . a few even violent. I frequently hid in the next room to listen when the fighting started. As much as I grew to hate their nasty bickering, I was somehow drawn into the arena when the boxing match started.

PollyJana felt it was my duty to try to stop my parents' constant fighting. Somehow, I needed to help control things at home. I just wanted all of us to be happy. I wanted us to live in the happy little town of *Janville*. I remember sweeping grass trimmings from our sidewalk in Houston as a nine-year-old after Mom mowed. She didn't ask me to do it; *PollyJana* just wanted Dad to be pleased with Mom when he got home, before he had his first drink.

A Man's Approval

As a kid, Dad's approval was very important to me. I could see his disrespect for Mom. I didn't intend to follow in her footsteps. I would learn to handle things in a way that would gain favor with the man of the house.

Dad didn't like whiners or wimps. As a kid, I didn't cry when I fell down and skinned my knees or elbows. I could bait my own fishhook at three. I didn't flinch when I went to the doctor for a shot. I didn't insist upon hugs and kisses from my parents. I was a faster runner than most of the boys in school. I wanted Dad's approval and I knew I wouldn't get it by demanding it. In some respects, I was Dad's first and only "son."

Dad valued his tough, stubborn, and self-sufficient little girl. When I taunted Dad by sticking my four-year-old foot in the neighbor's yard after he told me I couldn't go next door to play with a friend, my misbehavior led to a paddling. After I repeated the prohibited act only a couple of minutes later, leading to my second whipping, I think I gained Dad's begrudging respect. Later that year, when I voiced a rare complaint about a stomachache, Mom dismissed the problem, claiming it was probably due to an excess of Kool-Aid and birthday cake at a friend's party. However, Dad knew I wasn't a complainer. Our rushed trip to the hospital that afternoon resulted in emergency surgery to remove my appendix.

Dad also tended to defer to my tough stubbornness. He allowed me to escape the tedium of practicing piano, cello, riding, and dance, all activities that Mom set up during my early school years. As soon as I announced that I had lost interest in one of them, Dad would invariably let me off the hook, telling Mom, "Jane, there is no point in pushing Jan. She won't do it if she doesn't want to." He was right, making me right as well.

Running Away from Home

When we lived in Houston during my late elementary school years, I wanted to give my parents something more important to worry about than their intense dissatisfaction with each other. So, I devised a plan to run away from home. In my ten-year-old brain, I reasoned that they would be so worried about me, they probably wouldn't fight for several days.

Because I can be an obsessive planner, I had every intention of doing the runaway thing properly—you know, packing a suitcase, leaving a handwritten note, and so on. However, a particularly heated battle between my parents one evening preempted my carefully planned exodus.

Beth and I hid in the playroom under the pool table that evening listening to Mom and Dad's latest battle royal. As the yelling escalated, Dad burst unexpectedly into the playroom mid-fight and discovered our hiding place. Surprised, I spontaneously raced for the front door in my bare feet, sobbing uncontrollably. I ran down our long driveway toward the road as fast as I could, crying and praying I wouldn't step on any snakes. Dad jumped in the car, however, and caught me mid-driveway.

My hysterical confession about wanting to run away from home due to their constant fighting elicited a promise from Mom and Dad that they would stop the battling. The promise lasted . . . for a few weeks, until the ongoing alcohol abuse and relationship bitterness lead to the inevitable breach.

Arguing with an Alcoholic

Mom never got it. She never understood how to handle Dad's lectures and orders when he was tipsy. She tried to argue with him. Of course, she was never successful in winning the arguments, especially after her drinking began to muddle her already limited powers of persuasion.

Early on, however, I figured it out. You don't argue with an alcoholic. It's a battle you will never win. "Demon Booze" has already erased any rational thoughts that may have been previously possessed by your adversary. Rather, as I frequently instructed both Mom and Beth, just agree with whatever Dad says during the lecture . . . nod your head amiably, tell him you understand. Then go ahead and do whatever you intended to do in the first place. I grew to understand that, however thorough his original lecture, Dad's follow-up never was.

In fact, barring a serious contradiction of his instructions, Dad rarely revisited the issue. If he did, I would cry and fess up to the rule violation while usually noting that I merely wanted to spend time with my friends. "You know, Dad, the small handful of buddies I've been able to make in the couple of months *since our last move.*" My father's guilt over how his regular career moves uprooted my world usually resulted in a disciplinary capitulation in response to Jan's impassioned "friendship" defense.

The one topic where Dad's lectures actually made a difference on my behavior was the "boys and sex" talk, the one Mom never gave me. Despite my stubbornness and willingness to ignore Dad's other rules, his lecture on this topic not only controlled my teenage sexual urges but also, interestingly enough, actually helped encourage my early first marriage shortly after I graduated from high school.

Dad's sex lecture, delivered regularly between seventh grade my and senior year of high school, was direct and to the point. "Don't let boys touch you or talk you into having sex. They really don't care about you. All they are interested in is sex. They won't like you later. They will dump you afterwards. Kids at your age don't understand love." While his lectures on other topics may have gone in one ear and out the other, this one didn't, perhaps because I always wanted security and stability. I really wanted friends. I needed to be liked.

As a result, I shut down relationships with my high school boyfriends whenever their physical approaches went beyond making out and some mild petting. Dad's voice would inevitably sound the alarm bells in my mind. That boy I thought I was falling for instantly became a horned toad once he started pushing hard toward a physical relationship. I was a track star, dashing quickly away from every boyfriend who appeared to be motivated by sex.

Talking and Laughing: My Human Connections
I love to talk. Shortly after my first birthday, I earned the nickname "Myna Bird" from my parents because they claimed I could parrot back much of what I heard in adult conversation.

I have literally spent months of my life on the phone. I have always been willing to converse about everything, anything, and sometimes nothing at all, largely because I crave the human connection provided by friendship.

In a strange twist of fate, perhaps my parents' regular battles positively influenced my sense of humor. Even while I was in elementary school, I remember wanting to make people laugh. I often used my admittedly off-the-wall sense of humor to try to lighten things up on the home front and also in the classroom, much to the chagrin of my parents and teachers.

Given our family's frequent moves, I quickly learned that I had to use my sense of humor and be outgoing or I would be a very lonely kid. Dad's instructions on manners, including looking people in the eye, shaking hands, and remembering names, served me well. I was quick to reach out to others to initiate the conversation whenever I started at a new school or a new job.

The Ultimate People Pleaser

Even as a young kid, I was the ultimate people pleaser. What I didn't understand as a youngster was that my parents were also raising me to become a codependent—that is, someone who permits another person's bad behavior (often substance, physical, or emotional abuse) to run their life. Someone who then, in turn, becomes obsessed with trying to control and fix the abusive person.

Don't get me wrong: I'm sure my parents didn't want me to be a codependent. In fact, I doubt that either of them had even heard of the personality label. However, they didn't realize that their oldest daughter's desire to please people would transform her into becoming a slave to the same kind of chaos, anger, and substance abuse that controlled their dysfunctional marriage.

I grew up believing it was my responsibility to solve other people's problems, to keep them happy and help them avoid the consequences of their bad choices and actions. It was my duty to help Mom and Dad get along better. It was my obligation to enable and facilitate so that things would run more smoothly at home.

Further, given the constant challenges at home, I learned to try to fill my "happiness cup" by soaking in the approval of others. Unfortunately, my inordinate desire for approval and acceptance ultimately turned into an overpowering desire to control others as well. Let me explain.

Manipulation and Quid Pro Quo

We codependents typically learn how to manipulate others early in life. It's an acquired survival technique, one we often use to try to adapt to the chaos and dysfunction around us.

As a child, even as I tried to facilitate family harmony, I was also learning how to manipulate my Dad. I realized, again subconsciously, that I could use his alcohol abuse and/or his career ambitions against him to get something I wanted.

When Dad announced our move to Houston in 1962, I demanded a horse. I also got to choose all of the decorations for my bedroom. The move to New Jersey in 1964 brought my own bedroom downstairs, away from the family, along with a record player, a phone with unlimited calling privileges, and my own bathroom. Our eventual relocation to California in 1968 rewarded me with a swimming pool, input on the family car, full authority to decorate my room, and a new wardrobe.

Subconsciously, because I felt controlled, I guess I wanted to control. If I couldn't control the underlying circumstances that resulted in my life disruptions, perhaps I could manipulate the outcomes to obtain a corresponding reward: a quid pro quo—a trade-off that gave me something in return. Understandable? Sure. Pragmatic? You bet. A healthy approach to creating and sustaining authentic relationships? No way.

Jill and Jesus: Searching for My BFF

After my family followed Dad to his latest promotion in Los Angeles in 1968, I was bracing for a long junior year in California . . . another new school in a new state where I didn't know anyone. Fortunately, on one of my first days, I met Jill, a strong, passionate girl who later became my closest friend in high school. Jill was also the person who reintroduced me to Jesus. She was a Christian who later, during college, married a man who eventually became a Christian youth pastor.

In December 1969, Jill announced she was "born again" and she quizzed me about my faith. Drawing upon my admittedly rudimentary knowledge of the Bible, I was thankful at the time for Mom's bedtime prayers and my brief Sunday school exposure during my elementary school years. Jesus was the Son of God and He died on the cross for our sins, I casually responded to Jill. "Sure, I believe in God," I said. "So, what's the big deal?"

Jill was on fire with what she called the power of the Holy Spirit. She immediately invited me to attend some youth gatherings called Young

Life. Wanting to fit in and continue my friendship with Jill, I accepted the invite, without any real enthusiasm.

The kids at the Young Life meetings were nice and they seemed genuinely enthusiastic about their faith. However, after going a few times, I didn't feel any real emotional connection to the group or to my flannelgraph Jesus. Fortunately, when I bowed out, Jill didn't hold it against me, though her enthusiasm for her faith was undiminished.

At the end of my junior year of high school, Jill invited me to a Christian summer camp for a week. Again, I said, "Okay," my usual response to any social invitation. However, the weeklong camp experience did spark my curiosity about Christianity. Most of the kids in attendance were openly zealous about professing their faith. I remember thinking to myself, what is it that these people are so excited about? I tried really hard to feel the same passion even as I was asking myself the question, "Do they really believe this stuff?" Still, I guess I wanted some of whatever they had just to see if would work for me. Accepting the camp leader's invitation on the final day of camp, I decided to pray and ask Jesus to enter my heart.

Unfortunately, I didn't feel any different post-prayer than I had before praying. Somewhat disappointed, I decided I must not have gotten the "formula" right. Apparently, this being "born again" thing just wasn't for me.

Carrying Baggage into Adulthood

So, I left my early childhood and young adult years with some baggage, as we all do. However, the bags I lugged with me would prove very difficult to unpack . . . at least not until after I had already done some real damage to myself and those around me.

My baggage? The codependent daughter of alcoholic parents. The "rolling stone" kid who was determined never to move her family around the country like she was forced to do when she was a child. The kid who had heard about Jesus but who didn't really get to know Him. The people pleaser who wanted everyone to like her and to feel comfortable around her. The tough, headstrong girl who didn't need any help from anyone to decide what she wanted out of life. Interesting combination of character traits. Decades passed before I began to understand just how substantially these characteristics actually shaped my decision-making and my eventual life path.

Meeting Bill: Not Your Typical Guy
I met my eventual husband, Bill, at a party the night of my high school graduation ceremony in June 1970. He was twenty-two and I was eighteen. Bill had long hair and muscles. He also seemed somewhat detached and a bit mysterious. In my mature, teenage opinion, he was

"cool." He told me he was in college at UCLA working on a master's degree in math. Since math was never my fav topic in school, I was impressed with his apparent intellectual aptitude.

As we got to know each other, Bill told me a sad story about his difficult family life and his impoverished upbringing. His mom and dad divorced when he was five. Mom left town and took Bill's sister with her, but she dumped him with a great aunt. He saw his dad on weekends. Dad would bring him along to the local tavern, leaving Bill to play in the corner all day while Dad got smashed.

Wow, I thought, this guy has really had the odds stacked against him. His upbringing was very different from mine. Perhaps opposites do attract. Bill seemed impressed with where I lived; I was attracted to his story of neglect and poverty.

Bill wasn't like other guys when it came to the issue of physical contact while we were dating. We did some kissing, but he didn't push the sex issue. It was months into our friendship before we got intimate. In my teenage brain, he had passed the "Dad test." I believed that he really liked me for me, not just because I might become his sexual partner at some point.

Still, I also felt strongly that our relationship needed to be permanent once we became physical months after we first met. Even though my faith walk was still its infancy and Dad wasn't looking over my shoulder at this point, I wasn't about to test God or be a "sleep-around girl." Now Bill needed to be *the* one.

We had been dating for nearly a year when Bill offered me his ultimate compliment. One evening, after he had a few tall ones at a party, he told me that the real reason he liked me was I "fit in" with his friends. According to Bill, I talked to everyone, wasn't clingy, and didn't hang on him. He said he didn't like the "Suzy Pots and Pans"-type girls. Years later, I came to recognize that his supreme compliment that evening should have given me a reason to reexamine our relationship. My boyfriend liked hanging *around* me because he didn't have to hang *with* me. Still, at the time, in my teenage brain, I just wanted him to like me. I was proud of the fact that I wasn't a demanding princess.

Bill and I didn't have any real fights while we were dating. Still, I should have had my antenna up for other reasons. About three months into our dating relationship, I had a party at my house. Bill came late. Before he arrived, I noticed an attractive girl I didn't recognize come through the front door. When I introduced myself, she said she was "Bill's girlfriend from San Francisco," also telling me that she was staying at his house over the weekend. I tried to choke my look of surprise. I stayed deadpan even after she said that Bill told her about me, mentioning that he just liked me because I had "a nice house and money."

When Bill arrived, I quickly dragged him aside and asked about his "girlfriend." He cavalierly pushed my concerns to the side. He claimed that they had broken up some time ago because she was "too clingy." She came down for the weekend, only as a friend, and she was sleeping on his couch. Knowing how Bill felt about "Suzy Pots and Pans" girls, I was determined not to react. I played it cool. I nodded at his explanation and went back to my hosting duties. Sure, I felt hurt and uncertain, but I decided that I just needed to tough it out.

A few months into our dating relationship, I also discovered that Bill had quite a temper. The first time I witnessed one of his temper tantrums was during breakfast at the house he shared with his Great Aunt Mame after Bill discovered there was no more seedless blackberry jam in the refrigerator.

Bill blew up. His face was red and contorted. His fists were clenched as he yelled at his elderly aunt as though she had committed some horrendous crime. Sweet Aunt Mame, flustered and deeply apologetic, literally ran for her sweater and pocketbook so she could hobble to the store to get him his jam.

I was astounded . . . this guy was out of control over a jar of jam? Even coming from my dysfunctional home, I knew this wasn't appropriate behavior. Summoning some courage, I quickly interceded, telling Aunt Mame that she didn't need to run out to get it. As I frowned at Bill, I told her that Bill and I could walk to the market to get his blackberry jam, if he really needed it.

My mistake? Playing the enabler, sliding quickly into my well-re-hearsed, family-of-origin role as the codependent problem handler. I needed to solve Bill's problem. I needed to placate his anger. What I didn't do was confront his bad behavior or call it what it was—irrational and horribly inappropriate.

What lesson did I learn from the incident?? Discuss his temperamental behavior and seek changes with patience and reason? Address his irrational anger and the confrontation with prayer and Christian compassion? I didn't have the tools. However, I did make a mental note: NEVER, EVER forget that Bill wants blackberry jam—not jelly, not preserves, no seeds—chilled in the refrigerator and available at all times. Later, during my many years of marriage to Bill, we were never, ever out of seedless blackberry jam.

The Hernandez Group

During the time we were dating, Bill's best friends were a group of guys that congregated around a couple of brothers named Sam and Mark Hernandez. The Hernandez brothers came from a well-to-do family on the west side of LA. Sam was Bill's best friend. Sam was also the guy who led the group's parties, unabashedly encouraging others to get "messed up" and to "party hardy."

Bill apparently didn't want to disappoint on the party issue. He had a reputation within the group for knowing how to get really "messed up." When I joined the group as Bill's date, I indulged only in moderation. I was determined not to lose control like my parents often did when they drank. However, I also gave Bill his space to do his thing, a freedom he clearly appreciated.

The focus of the Hernandez group changed during Easter 1971. Mark Hernandez saw the movie *King of Kings*, and he decided the Christian story was actually true. Suddenly, Mark became the group evangelist, bringing us together with his guitar and Bible, not a case of beer and a bag of weed. He wasn't shy about telling everyone we needed to become Christians. His insistent appeals struck a chord with me, partially because of my earlier exposure to the Young Life group gatherings with Jill.

I remember thinking to myself, there must really be something to this Christian thing if these party people are buying into the story. Group activities quickly moved from partying and getting wasted to reading Scripture and singing songs about Jesus. Bill and I joined in. Soon, we were attending regular Bible studies at the Hernandez ranch and later at an old bank building that served as our informal youth "church."

During this encounter with the Christian faith, I honestly felt something different. I actually believed that I really had Jesus in my heart. Was it the setting? Perhaps that my boyfriend and his party dudes had now turned into Bible thumpers? Whatever the reason, I eventually laid claim to the label "born again," though I still couldn't point to a particular moment of my adult faith conversion.

As a nineteen-year-old, I became certain that Jesus was my Savior, God's Son who sacrificed Himself for my sin and my death. Still, I didn't feel the need to immerse myself in reading the Bible cover to cover. I also didn't feel that I needed to work on developing a personal relationship with Christ. At this point in my life, I was content with being part of a group that seemed to want something more than just our weekend parties.

Attending Village Bible Church

Within a few months of the religious conversion of the kids associated with the Hernandez group, Mark Hernandez was directing us to attend Village Bible, a new church outside of Moorpark. The church's young pastor, Pete Havland, offered a strong, conservative Christian message. Havland seemed "cool" but in the pulpit he paced, shouted, and pounded hard on the judgment that would befall those who failed to follow God's laws, including regular church attendance and evangelical outreach.

Perhaps as a result, congregants at Village were quick to adopt unique behaviors purportedly designed to exhibit contrition and

Christian loyalty—i.e., wives wearing hats as a sign of submission to their husbands. Further, Village members weren't shy about judging fellow members and other Christian denominations that didn't follow VBC's rules. As an example, years after leaving this small church, I finally accepted the reality that Catholics were, in fact, also Christian believers, despite the generally accepted view at VBC to the contrary.

When Bill and I started attending Village Bible Church, I remember constantly feeling that I wasn't doing enough to please God and to grow the kingdom. Still, we were helping around the church, as well as attending twice on Sundays and also Wednesday evenings. Trying to be "right" in God's eyes, and in the eyes of my VBC friends, became a preoccupation for me. Pleasing God and my fellow church members was my duty. I was pretty good at handling my duties.

Bill's Proposal and My Parents' Reaction: A "Marriage Made in Heaven"?

Bill proposed marriage at a party one night after a couple of drinks. He said he loved me and he reminded me again that I was cool, fit with his friends, and didn't hang on him like other girls. I said sure. I also asked him if he knew what he was saying and if he would remember it the next morning. He did.

Mom and Dad never really liked Bill. They didn't like his California-hippie look or his "other side of the tracks" story—one that signified, in their opinion, lack of potential. Of course, as a teenage girl smitten with her first real love, those were just two of the characteristics I found fascinating. Ready to jump out of the nest as a graduating high school senior, I probably also enjoyed the fact that my parents didn't really approve of my choice of boyfriend.

Ultimately, their opinion of Bill's potential was probably accurate. Shortly after we were married in 1973, Bill stopped working on his master's degree to become a local cop. His rationale? The job gave him weeks of free time to pursue his hobbies. Also, his retirement would be fully funded. The retirement part made sense. However, in retrospect, I probably should have thought a second time about his desire to maximize his time off work and, as it turned out, his time away from me.

Were Bill and I in love? Did I even know what a real love partnership should look like, given my minimal dating experience and my parents' dysfunctional marriage? Did Bill have the capacity to give to a marriage partnership? After all, he was dumped onto an elderly aunt by divorced parents as a young kid. Think we could have benefited from some in-depth premarital counseling?

Of course, none of those questions flitted across my radar screen at the time. I was looking forward to starting my adult life. Bill was a Los Angeles-area native. I was sure we wouldn't be moving around constantly like my family did. I believed that Bill and I would raise a happy family. He would be a great husband, a great father, and the spiritual leader of our family. Our kids would grow up in the church and in the same community. In the deep recesses of my youthful mind, my dream of *Janville* was starting to play out. I was excited.

Marriage, a Baby, and Attendance at VBC

Bill and I were married at Village Bible Church in January 1973 in front of our friends and families. We pledged ourselves exclusively to each other. We vowed to remain together as husband and wife "till death do us part." Unfortunately, over the years, I had numerous occasions to ponder whether Bill completely zoned out during the exclusivity portion of the vows exchange.

Bill and I moved into a small apartment in Porter Ranch after a brief honeymoon to Lake Tahoe. I was working at an upscale department store to help pay Bill's college tuition bills. I became pregnant within a week of being married. It was a shock. As a twenty-one-year-old girl, I wasn't keen about also becoming a mother quite yet. Still, I accepted my husband's statement that the pregnancy was probably God's will for our marriage. We had Mark, our first son, on October 28, 1973.

Bill attended church with me fairly regularly from the summer of 1972 until the fall of 1973. I loved sitting in church together. Still, I always had a gnawing sense that Bill wasn't really with me spiritually and emotionally. Soon, Bill wasn't with me physically either. He started missing church so he could go fishing and skiing, his secular religions.

In November 1973, Bill took a job as a weekend ski instructor at Mt. Waterman. The money he made teaching skiing really didn't make a significant difference in our budget. However, it gave Bill the excuse he apparently needed to miss church (and to return to his partying, though I didn't realize it at the time).

I was working full-time while also trying to raise our new baby. I bought into Bill's instruction that each of us needed to do "our part" to care for our young family. As such, I was quick to defend Bill's church absences when others at VBC would question his Christian commitment. Soon, members of the church and our social group were labeling Bill a "backslider" and "someone of the world." For his part, Bill began claiming that his friends had all turned into different people.

I was conflicted. I wanted to stand by my man. I became adept at making excuses for Bill's irregular church attendance. At the same time, my *Janville* family dream included regular attendance with my husband, the spiritual leader of our family. I felt anchored and stable when we were at VBC together, despite the rules-based, judgment-heavy message that generally echoed from the pulpit.

As Bill's absences increased, I begin to regularly remind him of how difficult it was for me to constantly attend church alone as a single mom. I felt judgment from our group. I was tired of making excuses for him. Inwardly, I was also beginning to question Bill's commitment to Christianity and to the church we had joined together.

The "Flexible" Fidelity Pledge

Other issues started to occur shortly after we were married that led me to start questioning Bill's commitment to our marriage. After he began teaching skiing at Mt. Waterman, there were nights when he wouldn't drive home, even though I was expecting him. His explanation was that he would be tired after teaching skiing all day and he would stay with another male instructor, who had an apartment outside of La Canada. Of course, *PollyJana* accepted that excuse without thinking . . . until a postcard addressed to Bill from a female ski instructor arrived in our mailbox one day. The card trumpeted that the girl had "a fun weekend" and that she couldn't "wait until next weekend."

When I confronted Bill about the card, he started yelling at me. "What are you doing reading my mail? Are you trying to check up on me?" and a host of other accusations. I was astounded and I burst into tears. I hadn't opened his mail. This was a postcard. It was from a girl who had obviously spent some weekend time with him and who was looking forward to more. What did I do wrong by bringing it to his attention? By asking a few questions?

Still, I quickly backed down. I accepted his explanation that it was just another instructor . . . just a casual friend . . . one who just sent a silly postcard. I had already developed a real fear of his angry tirades. Now, in the recesses of my mind, I was also starting to couple that fear with another, more significant one . . . a fear that, if challenged, he might get angry enough to leave Mark and me. It was definitely not part of my *Janville* dream that I would live life as a single, twenty-year-old mom.

One night, when Mark was only ten days old, Bill failed to come home. I was really struggling to care for our first baby. Now I was also worried sick about my husband. The incident went from bad to worse because my dad was visiting at the time. Dad suggested that we should start calling the local hospitals to see if Bill had been in an accident. Scared stiff, I nonetheless tried to downplay any concerns so my dad wouldn't start worrying about his daughter's marriage.

Bill eventually came home the next morning at 5:00 a.m. He claimed he had been studying at his professor's house and had fallen asleep. Dad made a point of telling Bill we had been up all night worrying about him. Dad also made a point of telling me, privately, that it wasn't right for Bill to act that way. Dad didn't know how insecure I already was by that point. And I couldn't tell him. I was his *tough* little girl.

Leaving VBC and the "Crabby Christians"

Our family attended Village Bible Church for almost five years. However, in year two, Bill's attendance was sporadic at best. It decreased substantially in years three and four, becoming nonexistent by 1978.

I tried to be faithful in my church attendance, but it was difficult, given my full-time work schedule, including occasional weekend shifts, and my child-raising responsibilities. I didn't have any social interaction with friends except at church. Bill was going to school during the week and he was teaching skiing on the weekends.

I valued several of the friendships we made as part of the Hernandez/ VBC group. I also wanted our son, Mark, to attend Sunday school. Still, I felt increasingly isolated and judged by other church members as a result of Bill's absences. Ultimately, a Sunday school pageant led to our family's permanent departure from Village Bible in December 1978.

Mark had a small part in the church Christmas program that year. Unfortunately, when it came time for him to appear on stage, he went AWOL. After the pageant, I spoke with his Sunday school teacher, Jillian, about my son's acting debut. Jillian made a point to tell me that, if our family had been attending church more regularly, perhaps Mark would have felt comfortable appearing on stage in the pageant. We left VBC that Sunday. I never looked back. I didn't need the judgment of those "crabby Christians" about our family's church attendance.

New Members at Christian Community Church

Despite our uncomfortable departure from Village Bible, church attendance was not optional in my mind; it was a "got to" responsibility. Having a church home remained part of my *Janville* dream even if Bill didn't share my level of commitment. In 1979, we started attending Community Christian Church and I enrolled Mark in Sunday school.

The anger I felt toward some of our friends at VBC was exceeded only by my anger toward Bill for his lack of spiritual commitment. On the other hand, I suspected that Bill viewed the judgment of our friends at Village Bible as his "get-out-of-jail (church)" card. He condemned his friends for their condemnation. I kept asking Bill to attend with me.

He kept offering his well-rehearsed menagerie of excuses, ranging from ski lessons to schoolwork to fishing to failing to get out of bed on time.

I joined a Bible Study Fellowship group for women hosted at CCC. I remained in the weekly study course for nearly five years. I relished the social time with my sisters. I also enjoyed the study talks followed by the small group breakout sessions. At this time, I also felt the need to dig deeper into my faith at CCC, particularly given my husband's abdication of his duty to be our family's spiritual leader.

In our second year at CCC, I became pregnant with Tommy—son number two. We had been trying to have a second child, but the doctors hadn't been optimistic, so this news was a real blessing. Still, I was also feeling increasingly lonely. By this time, I was attending church virtually on my own.

Nonetheless, I was excited about our pregnancy and I wanted to look forward with hope. Internally, I was also clinging to what I can only call the "desperate, pregnant Mom's plea"—i.e., if we have another baby, it will force my husband to be more committed to me and our family.

Tommy arrived on October 11, 1979. The hoped-for increased commitment didn't materialize for Bill, although it certainly did for me. When Bill wasn't working, he was fishing, hunting, skiing, drinking, and otherwise out of the house.

I was becoming increasingly frustrated. I was also tethered to my mothering duties, household tasks, church commitments, and teaching responsibilities at my part-time aerobics classes. I was also feeling more isolated from my husband. I wasn't happy with my life, but I didn't have a clue about how to resolve our problems.

My dissatisfaction eventually led to a prayer that I would end up praying for decades—a prayer I repeated endlessly, always before giving thanks for the blessings in my life. "Dear Lord," I would pray, "please work a miracle on Bill." After all, if Jesus could bring Lazarus back from the dead, he could certainly reform my selfish husband. As the days, months, and years passed without evidence of my requested miracle transformation, I didn't quit praying. I simply reasoned that

God couldn't hear me . . . perhaps I just needed to pray a little harder and a little louder . . .

Leading in the Church and Leading at Home

Feeling overburdened at home, I ultimately did what any good code-pendent in a similar situation would do: I added some additional duties at church. After all, I wanted to be liked. I needed to be needed. I wasn't good at saying no. Subconsciously, I probably also thought that more activities and good deeds would help fill the emptiness in my cup, be pleasing to God, and keep me from dwelling on my marital problems.

In 1980, I decided to become a leader in the CCC children's ministry. That meant I was teaching aerobics part-time, attending to church responsibilities on Mondays, Wednesdays, and Sunday mornings, raising an infant and a six-year-old, and trying to manage all of my duties at home, including caring for my husband. The good news? I really felt needed.

Our Family Celebrations: Happy Fifth of July

Holidays and family gatherings were rarely the happy *Janville* family times about which I fantasized. When the family was at home together on holidays while the kids were young, I would tread gingerly around the house, fearful of tripping a booby trap that might set off one of Bill's anger explosions, ruining the day.

Infrequently, a holiday dinner or family gathering would come off as I had dreamed it would. If we sidestepped a disaster, I would cling tightly to the memories of our family time and continue my self-talk that things were improving. More frequently, however, the holiday or family event would start or end with a blowup that would leave me picking up the kids, and the fragments of the day, in tears and all alone.

July 5, 1982 was one example of a holiday catastrophe that occurred during my first marriage to Bill. Since Bill generally worked on July 4, we would celebrate together as a family on July 5. I was preparing our holiday dinner of hamburgers, hot dogs, and the usual side dishes when Bill pulled open the refrigerator and demanded to know why there wasn't any beer. With three-year-old Tommy playing quietly in the corner of the kitchen, I briefly explained to Bill, without turning around, that we had beer in the garage but perhaps we were out in the refrigerator.

Kaboom. The bomb went off. "*No* cold beer in the refrigerator? Warm beer in the garage on a holiday?" Bill begin screaming his dissatisfaction while Tommy and I hid in the corner of the kitchen, wincing and trying to dodge his verbal spears. After a few minutes of venting his outrage at my idiocy and incompetence, Bill stormed out of the house, jumped into his truck, and sped off, ruining yet another family holiday.

The fearful minutes after his eruption turned into hours, and the hours into another sleepless night alone. I put the kids to bed and eventually laid down. I couldn't sleep so I went off into *Janland*, that place in my mind where I would worry incessantly. I ruminated about Bill's statements, his intentions, where he had gone, whom he was with, and when, or if, he might come home.

The familiar pattern was repeating itself yet again: the innocuous trigger event leading to the explosive, degrading monologue that labeled me as the reason for his anger. After the explosion, Bill would charge out of the house and I would spend the night alone. His anger and frustration would often serve as his self-justification to hit the bars and stay out all night.

By 10:30 a.m. the next day, Bill still hadn't come home. I strapped Tommy in the car and headed down to the local Lucky store to pick up some milk. My stomach was still tied in knots over the events on the fifth. As I drove past a local watering hole on my way to the grocery store, I spotted Bill's truck in the bar's parking lot.

Worried and now angry, I unstrapped Tommy from his car seat, saddled him on my hip, and headed toward the front door. Bill was sitting at the bar next to a girl and another off-duty policeman. My demand to know where he had been the night before triggered the next explosion. Bill jumped from his bar stool and literally dragged me toward the front door. The stench of stale beer on his breath was overpowering as he berated me. "How could you bring our three-year-old son into a bar?

Have you been spying on me again? Why would you drive around town aimlessly when there are things you should be doing at home?"

After putting the kids down later that evening, I cried silently in bed, again feeling alone and helpless. Swabbing the tears from my eyes, I also prayed my repetitive, seemingly worthless prayer. "Please, God, work a miracle on Bill to make him a real Christian partner." At the end of the prayer, I remembered to also thank the Lord for my blessings. After all, I had my kids. Further, at least when Bill was at work, I knew he couldn't be drinking, searching for female friends, or whatever else he would do on his free time to get away from me.

The fear and the painful knot in my stomach slowly begin to subside. Things could be much worse, I rationalized. We had some happy family times. I knew both of us loved the boys. Perhaps this was just my lot in life. I had to gut it out. Tough girls don't cry. I pushed away the tears so my mind could plan my busy, caretaker agenda for the next day. About an hour later, I fell into a restless sleep.

The next morning, after Bill came home, he continued his verbal assault on me. I had *embarrassed* him in front of his friends. He vehemently insisted that there was no reason for me to come into the bar because I could clearly see his truck was parked outside the bar. Since I could see his truck, there was no cause for me to worry or to wonder where he was at the time.

As his words hacked away at me, the tightness in my neck and stomach became almost unbearable. Over time, my physical reactions to his anger and to the constant uncertainty I felt in the relationship had become increasingly severe. I was now physically wired to react to this miserable environment of fear and hostility. I couldn't turn off my physical responses any more than I could turn off my emotional reactions.

Sure, the rational part of my brain was tugging at me to stand up— to refuse to again become a victim of Bill's angry and manipulative way of turning the tables by blaming me for his misbehavior and rage. However, once again my codependent guilt and fear triggers overpowered my rational thoughts. I actually felt ashamed. After all, I probably shouldn't have brought Tommy into the bar with me; I should have stocked the refrigerator with cold beer; I should have passed by the bar after I saw his truck was there . . .

Hold it together, Jan, I thought as I started to chant the usual mantra in my head. Don't make it worse by arguing with him. Turn the page. Get his breakfast, lunch, and dinner ready before he leaves for work tomorrow morning. Pretend happy. Make things "normal" again. Take care of the kids, the house, your duties. Be the good wife. Pray harder. I knew how to handle the situation. I was already nine years into our first marriage. This script had already been written.

Of course, this July 5 dinner wasn't an isolated incident. Over time, our family became conditioned to fear Bill's angry explosions. We learned to hide anything that might trigger those eruptions. As the kids grew up, the rules at home were clear:

Don't touch Dad's stuff

Don't make demands on his time.

Don't exhibit any emotion or weakness.

Stay out of the way if he is in one of his "moods."

Don't bother him if he has settled into his recliner.

Don't disclose any mistakes, including any purchases and/or any property damage to his things. Tell Mom so she can replace it.

We learned to communicate in covert hand symbols and ambiguous phrases to avoid confrontations, including, "I'd be careful about that," "You know how he is," "I wouldn't go there if I were you," "Better get that taken care of before you-know-who finds out."

The lessons Bill learned about anger? Bill had discovered, early in life, that a bully can often get his way. Over time, he became adept at using his volatile outbursts of anger to get what he wanted and to cover up his bad behavior. He learned he could even turn the tables on an adversary by making the object of his anger feel responsible for his temper tantrums. Through the years, Bill's anger was extremely effective at shutting down communication in our marriage—including any inquiry or investigation into his misconduct. Through the years, I learned about endurance and suffering in silence, attributes I convinced myself were Christian virtues.

Learning to Cope: Just Weather the Storm

When you are a victim of emotional abuse, you learn to do what is necessary to survive. Following a Bill eruption and faced with the prospect of days of ongoing anger, bitterness, and tension in our home, I generally turned into water, seeking the path of least resistance.

Let the issue go. Apologize for making him angry. Apologize for asking questions about his time away from home, including where he was and what he was doing. Apologize for any of my mistakes (i.e., failing to buy his shaving creme) or errors by the kids (i.e., losing a piece of his fishing equipment) that may have triggered the most recent outburst. Do your best to try to keep the household on an even keel. Try to keep things "normal" for the boys. Don't rock the boat.

Start the next day afresh. Get up in the morning and make him breakfast. Ask him gently if his coffee is warm enough. If he needs another piece of toast, make sure it is firm and extra crispy. Pack his meals for when he heads to the station. Make sure his clothes are washed and folded. Handle the kids' needs so they won't bother Dad. Keep the peace. Hang in there. Pray lots. Perhaps things will get better . . . someday.

Tearstained Letters of Loneliness

During the many years Bill and I were together, there were hundreds of evenings when he didn't call or come home as expected—often not until the wee hours of the next morning, if at all.

In an effort to entice Bill to come home as scheduled, I used a variety of tricks. I would tell him we were having something special for dinner (only his fav selections, of course), let him know that I had invited someone to stop by for a visit (someone he cared about, of course), or let him know that I could get my mom to sit the boys if he wanted to go to a movie (who was I kidding? He never did.). My ploys rarely worked.

On my evenings alone, I would worry incessantly, running off to *Janland* in my mind, even as I tried to act happy while reading stories with the boys before putting them to bed. After the kids went down, I would make sure I had Bill's dinner ready so he could warm it in the microwave when, and if, he came home. Then I would sob and write my letters to Bill . . . letters of sadness, loneliness, and bewilderment. I would leave each letter next to his now-cold dinner plate in the kitchen before I went to bed. Some mornings I would awake the next day to find the cold food, and the letter, untouched.

My letters were as repetitious as they were sincere. Why didn't he come home? Where was he? Whom was he with? Why didn't he want to be with me? Why wouldn't he call to let me know what he was doing? Why didn't he want to come home to be with the boys? Wasn't I attractive enough for him? What could I do better to make him want to come home and be with his family? Why couldn't he be like the other fathers and husbands we knew? Why didn't he care about me or my interests? How would he feel if I acted like he was acting? And so on . . .

Sometimes, I think Bill actually read the letters. However, he never responded to the questions in any of them, even if we talked briefly about the problem the next day. After offering a litany of excuses, in an effort to move past the issue, Bill would typically promise to call the next time he was going to be late. I hardly ever received the promised calls.

For years, I kept many of the letters he didn't immediately throw in the trash. Not sure why I didn't toss them. I guess rereading them provided me with an opportunity to cry . . . a second, third or fourth time . . .

The Devil in "Pretty" Clothes?

When attending my women's Bible Study Fellowship at CCC in the eighties, I frequently offered my well-rehearsed prayer for my family during our open prayer time. I prayed at least twice each month at Bible study, year after year, that God would do a miracle: that He would bring Bill into fellowship with Jesus and our church community. I also urged

Christ to make Bill our family's spiritual leader and my relationship partner.

Candidly, I was jealous of most of the other women in my Bible study. They seemed to have "real" *Janville* families . . . you know, the kind with husbands who attended church regularly, assisted in caring for the kids, carved out some "date time" for their wives, and were home at night. Week after week, I begged God to respond to my prayer to transform Bill. Week after week, however, there was no evidence of any change to Bill's heart or to his behavior. Candidly, my patience with God on this issue started wearing thin.

Wasn't I praying hard enough? Why didn't God listen to me? Why wouldn't He answer my prayers? Wasn't I upholding my end of the "good believer/good wife and mother" bargain? What kind of God would force me to live in this horribly difficult relationship, day after day, month after month?

I wanted answers to my prayers. Never a patient person, I felt God owed me a response. In March 1984, I believed I finally received some answers. However, they were not the responses I was expecting.

I had been teaching aerobics part-time since Tommy was born. In 1984, one of my classes was a lunch-hour group consisting of approximately fifteen businessmen. The class included a local CPA, John, who always anchored himself in the front row to my far left. I had fun with the group, and they seemed to enjoy themselves as we worked out and joked our way through class.

One evening in March 1984, Bill didn't call or come home . . . again. I was an emotional wreck. Had he been drinking? Was he with someone else? Had he been in an auto accident . . . the usual cadre of fears I tended to conjure up in *Janland* almost overwhelmed me. My neck was extremely tight and my shoulder numb—my common physical reactions to the stress in our marriage.

The next day, Bill still wasn't home, and my noon aerobics class was rapidly approaching. I slapped on some makeup and tried to dry my eyes as I pulled on my aerobics gear and packed Tommy in the car to head to the studio. I set up Tommy for playtime in the corner, put on my happy face, and somehow managed to struggle through the class without breaking down. However, after the class ended, I melted into a ball in the corner next to Tommy and just cried my eyes out.

After several minutes of uncontrolled sobbing, I looked up to see John striding up the stairs toward me. I was a physical and emotional mess, but he quickly put me at ease, gently asking if he could help in any way. While I had no intention of sharing my life struggles, the dam burst. As Tommy sat quietly playing with his Legos in the corner, all of the secrets I had so carefully hidden and locked inside—the secrets about Bill's drinking, girls, failing to come home, his lying, his angry outbursts—came pouring out.

John knew how to play the situation. He became a gentle, supportive new friend. He empathized and sympathized. He expressed his incredulity and anger at all the right times. Nearly an hour later, mascara stained and exhausted, I gathered up Tommy, thanked John for listening, and headed to the parking lot.

As I loaded Tommy in the car, I felt strangely relieved and validated . . . perhaps even euphoric. Someone else finally knew about Bill's horrendous behavior. Someone else knew my secrets. Someone else shared my anger at Bill's lack of commitment to me and our family.

In the spring of 1984, John and I started talking after class. He disclosed some of the problems he was having in his relationship with his fiancé. Candidly, it was nice to have a friend to share things with after years of trying to cover up and rationalize Bill's bad behavior. I began to look forward to my talks with John after class. I sensed that he felt the same way.

At Bible Study Fellowship, I continued to offer my standard prayer asking God to bring Bill into fellowship with Him and into relationship with me. However, increasingly my prayers lacked the intensity and urgency with which they were initially offered. I begin to wonder if God had placed John in my class to help me break out of the prison that had become my life. After all, I rationalized, God's plans for us are good, right? Perhaps John was the answer to prayer I had been waiting on.

Around that time, I met with Viola, our Bible study large group leader, to discuss our class, including my continuing prayers about Bill. I also briefly mentioned to her that I had met a "nice man" in my aerobics class who was aware of my situation and who had been very helpful.

Viola didn't pull any punches. She warned me that John was *my* answer, *not* God's response, to my prayers. She admonished me to be careful, observing that I was very vulnerable at this point in my life. She also noted that the devil sometimes put his gifts in "pretty" packages.

Viola wasn't my only advisor at the time. I was also counseling occasionally with Bonnie, a Christian therapist. She affirmed my belief that adultery was grounds for divorce. She also confirmed my suspicion that Bill was never committed to our marriage. However, she wasn't a bit supportive of my burgeoning friendship with John. In fact, she was very direct in telling me that I shouldn't be considering what she called a "rebound" relationship. She was certain that God was not directing me to run toward John.

While I didn't fully comprehend it at the time, the thoughtful observations of my Bible study leader and my therapist were really superfluous. They should have saved their breath. Jan was already moving full steam ahead on her own *Janplan*. Nothing either one of them said was going to change my direction.

After all, I really enjoyed just talking with John. He seemed to genuinely care about me as a person. It was obvious he didn't want me to suffer. I hadn't got that type of affirmation since before I married Bill in 1973. I was starved for attention.

Eventually, my weekly Bible study prayers about my husband changed substantially. I wasn't praying for Bill's heart and soul anymore. I started to pray more earnestly for concrete evidence that Bill was having an affair so I could leave him. My conservative Christian education taught me that adultery was the only grounds for a divorce. In my heart, I knew that Bill had violated this rule numerous times during our eleven-year marriage. However, I felt I needed hard evidence if I was going to walk away from the relationship without committing a major sin.

Divorce #1: Exchanging a Sin for a Sin

John and I tripped over the line and became romantic in late October 1984. I asked Bill for a divorce the next day. John hadn't asked me to marry him, but I knew that I had to get out of my marriage. I had a huge problem. Despite Bill's extensive history of drinking, women, lying, and emotional abuse, now I had also been unfaithful. I had to make it "right" with God.

Bill loved fried oyster sandwiches, something I detested. However, I made him one on October 30, 1984. The boys were out of the house as I sat across the table watching him chomp on his favorite treat. About midway through, I asked him for a divorce. The oysters didn't cause the muffled choking sound he made halfway through his sandwich.

Bill got misty. He said he couldn't believe I actually wanted a divorce. He promised he would change. After some pleading, he pulled out the anticipated "God" arguments that he had used so frequently during our eleven-year marriage to keep me in check. "Jan, we were married in the church. God gave us our sons. Therefore, God wants us to be together forever, regardless of any challenges." Bill said he was sorry and that I had to forgive him, just as God had forgiven each of us for our sins.

I sat motionless and emotionless. I had heard it all before. When his pleas were finally done, I looked him in the eye and told him I couldn't do it anymore. I reminded him of the dozens of times over the years when I had complained that I couldn't stand his not coming home, his lying, and his uncontrollable fits of anger. I asked him to leave. He packed a bag and left that evening after the kids went to bed.

About a week after his fried oyster sandwich, Bill called me. He said he wanted to get back together. I learned he had been staying with the Hernandez family, though I was certain he hadn't even talked to any of them in several years.

Now Bill claimed he was a "new person," a "changed man." Acknowledging that he needed to confess to be forgiven, Bill offered a big one. He told me that he had an affair with our neighbor, Laurie, that lasted for "some time," though he also claimed he had terminated it a few months earlier.

Bill's confirmation of the relationship with Laurie affirmed a suspicion I had been chewing on for years. At this point, however, I wasn't a bit impressed with Bill's expression of contrition. I knew he wouldn't be truthful. Further, he had just sprung open the door of my prison cell. His confession meant I could get the divorce I had been praying about for months. I believed God had answered my prayers.

Still, despite acknowledging his sin, Bill wasn't going to give up easily. He immediately went back to Village Bible Church. He even asked Pastor Havland to reach out to me on his behalf.

The pastor called me. He told me I had to take Bill back since he had confessed and asked for forgiveness. Havland stressed that Village Bible didn't believe in divorce, regardless of the reason. In fact, he told me I didn't have any choice in the matter, if I was a true Christian. In support, he cited the example of a couple that attended Village Bible. According to Havland, the husband, who had committed adultery and been forgiven by his wife eight times, was also entitled to her forgiveness on the ninth occasion as well.

Are you serious? Really? I hadn't had any contact from the VBC people for years. They had condemned our family. They refused to offer me any support during the time Bill was purportedly "backsliding" in his church attendance. Yet now their pastor was commanding me to ignore Bill's repetitious infidelities and lies in favor of continuing a relationship that had never been a real marriage.

I hung up on Havland. Some other Village Bible people who called me later with similar admonitions received the same reaction. Emboldened by my budding relationship with John, I had no time for Bill's ploys, nor those of his "Bible-thumping surrogates" who were trying to shame me into staying with him.

Sure, I was fighting some heavy guilt associated with how I was leaving the marriage. Nonetheless, I didn't buy the "seventy times seven" forgiveness commandment from the Bible that Bill recited in his defense. By this time, I honestly didn't feel that it applied to my situation.

I had simply suffered too much. There was no way that Bill and his buddies were going to guilt me back into this miserable marriage. I was mad at my husband, mad his puppet church people, and also mad at God.

"Biblically Based" Arguments to Control and Intimidate

Bill often used his unique understanding of the Bible as a tool to control and intimidate me. When confronted with his latest lie or other transgression, he would typically draw upon select bible verses and teachings to try to make me feel guilty for ever considering divorce, including:

- *Didn't God bring us together to become one?*
- *Didn't Christ intend that nothing should sever our marriage, including some occasional sins and mistakes by one spouse or the other?*
- *Wasn't the apostle Paul granted forgiveness and grace when he failed to do what was right, as a result of the sin "living" in him?*
- *Aren't all of us "slaves to sin," as Paul once wrote?*
- *If someone suffers from a "disability" such as alcohol abuse, isn't it right to forgive the person while also recognizing that a disabling disease actually controls their behavior?*
- *Isn't it true, as the apostle Paul said, that nothing, no sin or mistake, can ever separate us from God's love?*
- *Didn't our pastor at Village Bible teach us that even affairs require forgiveness and grace?*
- *In fact, didn't Jesus command us to forgive one another seventy times seven times?*

The list went on and on. Bill was very adept at using our early, legalistic Christian training at VBC to pound into my head that I had no choice but to remain with him, regardless of his transgressions. He would often protest, "God brought us together. You are a sinner if you leave." What Bill never seemed to consider were the other Christian commandments that also required him to repent, to turn around, to walk away from his sin:

Well then, should we keep on sinning so that God can show us more and more of his wonderful grace? Of course not! Since we have died to sin, how can we continue to live in it? . . . We know that our old sinful selves were crucified with Christ so that sin might lose its power in our lives. We are no longer slaves to sin.

—Romans 6:1–2; 6 NLT

Those who are dominated by the sinful nature think about sinful things, but those controlled by the Holy Spirit think about things that please the Spirit. So letting your sinful nature control your mind leads to death. . . . Those who are still under the control of their sinful nature can never please God.

—Romans 8:5–8 NLT

Jesus said to the people who believed in him, "You are truly my disciples if you remain faithful to my teachings. And you will know the truth, and the truth will set you free."

—John 8:31–32 NLT

"If you keep my commands, you will remain in my love, just as I have kept my Father's commands and remain in his love."

—John 15:10 NIV

"He who has My commandments and keeps them is
the one who loves Me; and he who loves Me will be
loved by My Father, and I will love him and will disclose Myself to him."

—John 14:21 NASB1995

"Anyone who doesn't love me will not obey me. And
remember, my words are not my own. What I am telling you is from the Father who sent me."
—John 14:24 NLT

In Bill's world, his continual sinning was not only inevitable but also
totally acceptable. Do the bad deed, confess, ask for forgiveness, and
great news! You are free to purposefully and intentionally go and do the
same sin again . . . and again . . . and . . .

My Escape to John
Bill and I were divorced on June 10, 1985. John and I were married a
week later. Mom took the boys while John and I honeymooned in Santa
Monica.

I should have been ecstatic at this point in my life. I had finally broken away from the fear, the lies, the abusive anger, and the manipulation that had imprisoned me during my entire eleven-year marriage to
Bill. I was certain that God had granted my wish for the evidence I
needed to get a divorce.

I also believed that, for husband number two, God had sent me a
stable man who was willing to attend church with me. My next *Janplan*
was in process. John and I took the New Members class at church before we were married. I had made it clear to John that I wasn't going
to marry a nonbeliever. However, our marriage ended before we ever
really started attending church together.

Our honeymoon was a disaster. John got the flu. That was un-
fortunate, but how he handled it was worse. The guy started timing,

charting, and discussing every trip he made to the bathroom. He asked for Cream of Wheat cereal and then complained that I didn't make it "lumpy" like his mother did. When we finally got an afternoon on the beach, he again pulled out his timer and began instructing me when to turn over and when to get out of the sun. He berated me for having a brief, friendly conversation with a sanitation worker emptying trash outside our hotel room. Later, he volunteered to extract a minor blemish on my face that he apparently found unsightly.

This guy had some serious control issues. By the time we were headed back to Los Angeles, I had come to the realization that I probably made a serious mistake by jumping from Bill to John. Was it possible that the "don't rebound" advice my Bible study leader and my Christian therapist had offered was on target?

The Annulment Cake

Once John and I returned home from our honeymoon, I immediately called the pastor who married us at CCC for an appointment to speak with him. I had decided to seek an annulment of my marriage to John after only twelve days of marital "bliss."

As I prepared for the meeting, it dawned on me that I had told the pastor that I was already divorced from Bill when I asked him to perform the marriage ceremony for John and me. In reality, the divorce from Bill had not become final until just one week before the pastor pronounced John and me "husband and wife." Now I was going back to the same clergyman to ask him to help me get an annulment, after a mere two weeks of marriage to John.

Ummm . . . probably didn't sound very good. So, Jan decided she needed another *Janplan*. Ahhh, let's see . . . perhaps I needed a peace offering to help facilitate a successful meeting. Ok . . . I'm an accomplished baker. I decided to make a cake for my minister.

Pastry in hand, knees shaking, I went to the pastor's office at the appointed time. First, I came clean about the timing of my divorce from Bill. Then I requested his assistance to get an annulment of my less-than-two-week marriage to John. I never got to the cake presentation.

The pastor swiveled his chair, turning his back toward me, and he refused to rotate back around. I eventually decided, after staring at the back of his head for a couple of minutes, that the meeting was probably over. I left, clinging to my cake. Because John wouldn't agree to an annulment, I called my attorney and asked her to file the divorce papers.

The Power of Guilt and Shame

A normal person might have concluded that this would have been a good time to head home, take care of the kids, return to Bible study, and schedule daily sessions with my therapist. Not me. My guilty conscience already had me replaying Bill's "God" arguments in my head. Jan, the people/God pleaser, needed to make things right. I needed a new *Janplan*. As Bill had repeatedly preached, we were married in the church, we were blessed with two wonderful boys, and on and on. I rewound and replayed his arguments and pleas over and over. Perhaps it really was God's plan that we should always be together.

Guilt over my ill-fated relationship with John also had my head spinning. The admonitions of the Village Bible people about the sacred institution of marriage were clamoring in my brain. Shame over the way I left Bill overwhelmed me. Simultaneously, I began to glorify the few good memories I had of my time with Bill. After all, we had some good family vacations, Bill kept food on the table, there was familiarity in my routine as the spouse of a public safety officer, Bill taught the boys sports, etc.

I called Bill the day after I filed for divorce from John. Perhaps he was right that God wanted us together . . . perhaps I had been too hasty in fleeing when he said he finally wanted to try to save our marriage . . . perhaps he was right that I needed to forgive him, regardless of the circumstances. Bill, of course, agreed that our reconciliation would be the right thing to do in God's eyes. He promised he would do "whatever it takes" to make it right with me and the boys. Ok, Jan, time to get back to "normal."

Of course, I wasn't an idiot. I would make him agree on some critical relationship changes. No more women. No more lying. He would come home every night. He would go to church. He would also cut back on his drinking. We needed to be clear about the terms that were fundamental to our reunion.

Also, as part of our reconciliation, we agreed that, because Bill had the Fourth of July off this year, he would come over for dinner and we would take the boys to the fireworks. I played up Daddy's return with Mark and Tommy. We were all excited for our planned Fourth of July family celebration. The bells in *Janville* were ringing again.

The Fourth of July holiday arrived but Bill didn't. Not in time for dinner, not after dinner, not even in time to take the boys to the fireworks. Not until after midnight, accompanied by the strong odor of alcohol. Earlier that evening, for the umpteenth time, I had made up an excuse for the boys to cover for their father's conduct, telling them that Dad had to go to work and couldn't be with us.

I was furious at myself for ever believing that I could trust this man to do what he said he would do. I booted him out again. In tears, I once again tossed and turned in bed until I fell into a fitful sleep in the early morning.

Things were a bit complicated at this point. My dad was scheduled to fly into California from Florida to meet John, my new husband, on July 10, 1985. Awkward . . . still, I knew I had to get through his visit. After all, I was Dad's tough girl, I was Bill's tough girl; I had to be that tough girl. Act happy and deal.

As soon as Dad arrived, I pulled him aside and told him I had made a mistake in marrying John (probably true). I also told him that I might be getting back together with Bill (probably not true). Dad was confused and not very happy. Ditto for me, Pops. Still, I had to make it appear that I had it together so Dad could enjoy his time with the boys and me. Put the problems in a drawer and close it . . . for now . . .

I went back to Bonnie for some counseling. I felt I needed some Christian therapy after deciding to leave John but before returning to Bill. Bonnie was gentle with me. However, she also tried to help me realize that returning to Bill, in light of our extensive, problematic history, probably wasn't going to be a successful option, for a host of reasons.

One of those reasons, according to Bonnie, was that I never really had a marriage with Bill because I was filling the role of the mother who abandoned him. I was his caretaker and his disciplinarian, not his wife. He wanted to sneak away from me to "play." I was also the primary target for his adolescent-like anger eruptions, she pointed out.

Bonnie used a simple example to help me understand that Humpty-Dumpty wouldn't fit back together. "Say you start scrambling some eggs, Jan, and then you suddenly decide you want to fry each egg sunny side up . . . you can't put them back in the shell to start over." Further, she homed in on my guilt-ridden receptivity to Bill's repetitive arguments that God demanded we stay together because we were married as Christians in the church. If that argument is determinative, she wondered, how was I going to reconcile divorcing John? After all, we were also married as Christians in a Christian church.

My head was rotating in circles on top of my neck by this time. I was trying to reconcile my confused heart with the advice of my therapist and the rules-based teachings of Village Bible Church. It seemed to me that whatever direction I turned, I was going to sin. If that was the case, I decided I just needed to make a plan—I needed another *Janplan*. Ultimately, I decided to go with my gut, the organ that, unfortunately, directed most of my important life decisions over several decades.

John: Take Two

In August 1985, I called John and told him to come back. He agreed, noting that he knew all along that I wasn't really going to return to Bill. I even bought a house for John and me, rationalizing that I was certain we could work things out this time. After all, John was a stable professional, he wouldn't cheat on me, he wasn't a big drinker and . . . umm . . . well . . . I really liked his sister and his mom.

However, within a few months John's controlling nature again became a problem. He wanted me to dress more flamboyantly, didn't want me to joke or be myself in front of his friends, and he occasionally yelled at my boys without any apparent reason. In a short time, I knew

I couldn't live with his need to remake me and our family to fit the image he wanted.

The Reprise . . . Marriage #2 to Bill

After my divorce from John became final, I married Bill for the second time in the fall of 1986 after I discovered I was pregnant for a third time. Talk about a sign from God . . . my doctor had previously told me that my second pregnancy was against "all the odds." So, what was this third one? Perhaps a heaven-sent miracle?

At this point, Mark was twelve, Tommy was six, and now I was going to have another baby with Bill. I was a part-time aerobics instructor with no savings account and no one to rescue me. Maybe God really did want us to be together?

Our Hawaii Honeymoon and Janine

Bill and I were remarried in Hilo, Hawaii on October 9, 1986. Our honeymoon was awkward. Bill was drinking and I couldn't have a drop, due to my pregnancy. I remember being thankful when our plane landed in Los Angeles after the trip. I wanted to get back to our "normal" life, including time with the boys.

When we arrived at my house, Bill quickly unloaded my bags and jumped back in his truck to drive away. Surprised, I stopped him and asked where he was going. His reply, that he was going back to the house he had been renting, caught me sideways.

"You're not staying here with me and the boys now that we're married?" I asked in amazement. "What am I supposed to tell Mark and Tommy . . . that Daddy doesn't live with us anymore, even though we are remarried? Aren't you even going to come in and help me put them to bed?"

Bill responded with a negative shrug. He claimed he was tired, he had to work the next day, and he was going home to bed. After he drove off, I made up excuse #556 for the boys about Dad's sudden, urgent call to work that evening. I put them to bed, cried, and then returned to *Janland,* chasing the morass of conflicting thoughts that were racing around my head. Around eleven o'clock, however, my suspicious thoughts about Bill's intentions won out over my guilt-ridden "just trust and do the right thing for the boys" thoughts.

This guy was up to something. Racking my brain, I remembered that, months prior to our getting back together, Bill had been dating someone named Janine. Was she the reason why he was in such a hurry to dump me off after our honeymoon trip? Checking on the boys to make sure they were sound asleep, I jumped in my car shortly after 11:00 p.m. and a drove a few minutes over to Bill's house to see if he had returned home as he said he was going to do. No evidence of his truck. No evidence of Bill.

The next morning, I called the station after he started his shift to speak with my new husband. I asked Bill what he did after he left me the previous evening. He repeated his claim that he went home to bed. I told him that I had driven by his house and he wasn't there.

Bill blew a gasket. After his explosion caused him to run out of breath, I asked him if he had been with Janine. Caught off guard, he vehemently denied any relationship. Then he went on another rant about my repeated "false accusations," my lack of trust, and my uncalled-for investigations. Near the end of this speech, however, he flippantly invited me to go ahead and call Janine, if I didn't believe him.

As good as he was at covering his tracks, Bill made a grievous error on this one occasion. He obviously forgot that, when we were divorced, he had given me Janine's phone number. Months earlier, after Tommy had injured his leg, I needed as many communication avenues as possible to try to contact Bill during our son's recovery. I still had Janine's phone number, though I had never previously used it. This time I did.

Janine and I had a short but cordial call. To put it bluntly, she was stunned to learn that Bill and I had remarried, that I was pregnant, and that we had just returned from our honeymoon the same evening he appeared at her house for their most recent slumber party. "Good luck with that . . ." were her closing remarks as we ended our call.

I was near the end of my rope, physically, emotionally, and spiritually. I felt trapped again by Bill's deceitful abuse and by life circumstances.

"Mom" was about to again become "Mommy." My family needed me to come through for them even if my husband was never going to come through for us. I had to suck it up . . . I needed to be Dad's tough little girl once more.

At this point, I didn't want to let anyone know that I was a Christian. Given my dysfunctional marriages, I didn't want to give my faith a bad rep. Most of my friends and family wouldn't even talk to me when I told them I was back with Bill again. I was even too embarrassed to return to my therapist. I had no one to talk to but my kids and, of course, they needed protection, not justification.

Church as Punishment

Between 1986 and 1991, I used church attendance at CCC as periodic punishment for Bill. Whenever he would act out, I would get him to agree to the now repetitive promises: No more drinking or girls. Come home on time. Attend church regularly or I'm leaving. After all, these were the things that the husbands in my dream village of *Janville* did. I wasn't asking for perfection, just some stability and respect.

After Sam was born in March 1987, my frenetic routine of meeting family needs helped me periodically forget that I was miserable in my second marriage to Bill. I have always been a high-energy person. I doubled down on my household care activities, believing that the whole world would come to a screeching, calamitous halt if I didn't handle everything perfectly. My life was all about taking care of my family.

I continued to make Bill his breakfast, lunch, and dinner, washed and ironed his clothes, cleaned the house, got groceries, did the gardening and home repairs, and handled all family plans, financials, and outside communications while also raising the kids and working part-time. School lessons with the boys, attending parent–teacher conferences, working on school projects, disciplining the kids, you name it.

Bill's only real interests were teaching the kids sports and fishing, the activities that he also enjoyed. This was the singular family area where he would give of his time freely. He did it well. The boys were talented and they enjoyed the sports Dad taught them.

Bill wouldn't do anything around the house unless I demanded it, and then only begrudgingly and with much complaining. While Bill's drinking didn't seem as flagrant in the year or two after Sam was born, it never really stopped. He just became a bit more adept at concealing it.

The Call Back to Chaos

On March 16, 1990, my *Janville* world came crashing in again. The boys and I had just returned from a trip to the grocery store. I was bringing in bags of groceries with one arm while extracting Sam from of his car seat with the other when the home phone rang. After barking orders to the boys, I picked up the phone and was greeted by a caller named Cecily Rafter, who identified herself as "Bill's girlfriend."

Instantly, the all-too-familiar panic gripped my neck, throat, and shoulder as I started to comprehend the nature of the call. I yelled at Mark to keep an eye on his younger brothers and I raced to the bedroom to pick up the extension phone.

Cecily told me that she and my husband had been seeing each other for some time. Recently, some of Bill's behaviors caused Cecily to suspect he might not be telling her the entire truth about his marital status. She called the police station and a station dispatcher confirmed that Bill was, in fact, married to "Jan," so Cecily tracked down our home number to inform me of the affair. Cecily also wanted to make it clear that she would *never* have gotten involved with Bill if she had known he was married.

I was sitting on the floor of the master bedroom by this time, physically shaking. My pulse was racing as I tried to quietly inhale and exhale to avoid a complete meltdown. I mouthed a virtually soundless "thank you" at the end of the call and struggled to return the extension phone to its base.

Once again, Bill was back to his escapades. Once again, this victim had no one to talk to about our latest marital crisis. My family and friends had warned me explicitly not to go back.

After the boys went to school the next day, Bill and I danced our now very familiar tango as I confronted him about his latest dalliance.

His first dance step in response was to offer the usual shallow, made-up excuses (i.e., he didn't really like her that much, he had tried to break it off, etc.). His second, all-too-familiar move was to beg for forgiveness, claiming he would do "whatever I wanted" to make things right. He didn't immediately toss out the "God card" this time, probably sensing that it might ring a bit hollow, given the overwhelming evidence of his most recent misconduct.

When it was my move, I admittedly wanted to humiliate him. Even as I lashed out, I was also frantically trying to identify in my mind the next step for the boys and me. In my anger, I reasoned that this time would be different. I wouldn't act happy to avoid the tension of an anger-filled household. This tough girl was going to use her toughness on Bill. He darn well better toe-the-line this time. And I really meant it (or, in retrospect, I'm sure I meant it, at least for a few hours).

Taking Bill Back . . . Again

Over the next few days, I made Bill promise to quit drinking completely and go to AA. No more female friends, no phone numbers, and no incidents where he failed to come home. Further, he would go to church with me *and* he would help around the house and in the yard, without complaining.

To my surprise, Bill actually upheld most of his end of this bargain for about two-and-a-half years. He was sporadically helping some around the house, including one quick cleaning of the infamous black hole we called the garage. Further, we attended church infrequently, at least when the multiple weekend sports activities of the kids didn't interfere.

Still, Bill continued to focus exclusively on his hobbies and his interests. He didn't make any attempt to be in "relationship" with me. This new Bill was a far cry from the ideal husband that lived with me in my *Janville* family fantasy. Still, it seemed he wasn't drinking or up to his other activities, so I told myself I should be thankful for a step in a positive direction.

My problem was I just couldn't try. I was abrupt and short with Bill. I didn't want to make any effort. I was dulled by the pain I had experienced over the years. It was all I could do to try to make our home life appear as normal as possible for the boys. My heart and my head were checked out.

Also, Bill exhibited no desire to be the spiritual leader for our family and he avoided attending services, even after the Cecily incident. Unfortunately, in 1991, some staff members at CCC handed him the ammunition he needed to walk away from Christianity, once and for all.

Church Sex Scandal Rocks CCC

In 1991, CCC and several western LA suburbs learned about a sex scandal involving the church's senior pastor and a female Bible study leader. Because the pastor was an excellent preacher and a highly visible member of the community, the affair caught both the media and Bill's attention. He tossed the local newspaper at me one morning with the snide, self-congratulatory exclamation, "So here's what your good Christians at CCC are up to . . . the hypocrites."

I was devastated. For years I had been praying to have God transform my husband, to make Bill a caring, faithful man and the spiritual leader of our home. For years I had been praying that my entire family could worship together each Sunday at church. Now, in my mind, all my prayers, all my arguments urging Bill to be a leader for our family, all my prayers for God's intervention in our relationship, had been shown to be just a bunch of hot air.

How could I pray that Bill would finally stop screwing around when the senior pastor of our church was doing the same thing? How could I pray for pure hearts with my Bible study sisters when my study leader was having an affair with our head pastor? Was Bill right that even the seemingly "good" Christians were probably all just hypocrites?

Unfortunately, my faith wasn't deep enough at the time to separate the isolated but sinful conduct of two imperfect church leaders from the truth and sanctity of the Bible's message. After all, Bill constantly begged for forgiveness using the same argument . . . "I'm a flawed believer but you need to forgive my sin and take me back." At this point, I was so disillusioned that I couldn't handle it.

I essentially divorced myself from my prayer life and from the church. For his part, Bill actually seemed somewhat content for short while. At least now he didn't need to make any excuses to cover his disinterest in church. The boys were also fine with sleeping in and pursuing their sports activities on Sundays. I was the one who felt a void. I was aimlessly wandering now. My periodic church refuge, my oasis in the spiritual desert of my life, had been shown to be a mirage.

Filling My Spiritual Void

How could I fill the emptiness I was feeling in my life? What could I do to feel more happy and fulfilled? I obviously needed another *Janplan*. So, I did what many women do to fill the void: I went shopping.

In addition, my mom and I were becoming increasingly involved in our small side business, purchasing and refurbishing antique furniture and other items. I begin to devote my free time to the hunt, the buying and the resurfacing of the furniture. I could lose myself for hours when I was in my mom's backyard shop stripping, sanding, staining, and varnishing items for resale. At this point in my life, my refurbishing work was the perfect escape from my imperfect marriage. I didn't know how to renovate my marriage, but I did a great job renovating furniture.

Isolation from Family and Friends

From the time Bill and were first married, I felt isolated and alone when trying to cope with our relationship problems. Like many victims of abuse, I was too embarrassed to turn to my family and friends to talk about our difficulties. After all, I wasn't a physical abuse victim; my injuries were "only" emotional ones. I didn't feel my situation really merited the attention and support of others.

I was also convinced that telling family and friends about the abuse would probably make things worse. Bill would get retribution. I decided there was nothing to be gained by being vocal. Shut up and suffer in silence. The Jan that talked about everything and anything wasn't talking about this area of her life. Act happy and perhaps you will eventually be happy. Fake it till you make it.

My guilt-ridden early Christian education and my codependent nature also contributed to my isolation. Based on my understanding of my spousal obligations, I couldn't help but feel I was failing as a Christian wife. I simply needed to do a better job. I needed to make Bill happy somehow. I needed to pray harder to turn the relationship around. As a codependent, I felt I needed to get control of the situation to make it better. Bill was a puzzle that needed to be solved. His behavior was a problem that needed fixing—and I liked being needed. I liked trying to fix things.

My friends and family could see glimpses of my unhappiness, even if they only knew a handful of the details about Bill's conduct. Few were ever Bill supporters. So, I concealed most of the details about our relationship, partially to protect him and partially because of my embarrassment and confusion about our situation. I lived in isolation, particularly in the first two marriages, hiding our problems. At times, the loneliness and pressure were almost unbearable.

More *Janplans* ... Different Facts, Same Results

Remember the Bill Murray movie *Groundhog Day*? At this point in my life, I was living it. No matter what *Janplans* I tried, the results were always the same. In my marriage, every day seemed like a repeat of the one before. Despite my repetitive efforts to change Bill, I wasn't seeing the payoff I felt I deserved. Of course, I wasn't working nearly so hard on changing Jan or on honestly seeking God's intervention in my life. I had convinced myself that Jesus needed to address Bill's issues. Further, Christ obviously needed my help to get it done. So, I continued to shoot at a moving target while also puzzling over why God wouldn't show up for me.

An Old Friend Resurfaces

In the later part of 1991, Bill missed one of Tommy's baseball games. As the game ended and just as I was about to explode with anxiety, Bill came running up, smiling and spewing apologies for his late arrival. He claimed he had just run into an old friend, Frank Rewes.

Back in the Hernandez group days, Bill and Frank were fishing buddies. I had gotten to know Frank fairly well during that time. While Frank had not jumped into religious studies with the rest of us, he was a member of the group and someone that both Bill and I enjoyed.

About a week later, Frank came to dinner at our house. The following week, Frank called to inquire about the brand of a fishing knife Bill had identified at dinner. Frank wanted to purchase one for his father.

Bill wasn't home at the time, so Frank and I spent the next hour on the phone together. About halfway through the call, Frank asked pointedly, "So how are things going with Bill?" He got a much longer and more detailed response than he was expecting. I hadn't anticipated providing a flood of information, but Frank was someone with whom I had always felt comfortable. I really needed someone to listen. Frank did.

I told him about the nights Bill didn't come home, the alcohol, the angry outbursts, and many of the other details about our relationship. In light of my offering, Frank felt comfortable sharing as well. He knew a lot about Bill's past party activities. By the end of the call, Frank and I had formed a special bond cemented by our mutual knowledge of the inappropriate conduct by his friend, my husband. Frank also made it clear that, at this point, he held no special affection for Bill, especially in light of how he had apparently treated me over the years.

Frank was easy. He was familiar. He was a cop. He enjoyed fishing, hunting, skiing, walking, and refurbishing furniture. He had been estranged from his wife for over nine years, though they had never gotten a divorce. He made it clear during our call that he always had an interest in me. We begin talking regularly on the phone.

By this point, my oldest, Mark, had graduated from high school. Bill was still drinking, controlling, and periodically exploding in anger at all of us, but at least he was coming home at night. He must have felt that he was fulfilling his duties as husband and father. However, I had lost all confidence that our marriage could ever be salvaged.

I didn't have a *Janplan* to run to Frank. I just knew it felt wonderful to finally let out the secrets I had been living with over the past seven years. Frank was a kind, willing listener. He was supportive. He was comfortable and I knew he liked me. It felt good to talk with him. Even when we shared a hug after sandpapering a piece of his furniture in the shop, it somehow didn't seem wrong or forced. Of course, neither did my relationship with John at the time it started.

Once again, Jan had a problem she didn't want to acknowledge. I wasn't in relationship with God. I wasn't even praying at this point in my life. Candidly, I didn't even feel the need to "check in" periodically with Jesus. After all, as I subconsciously reasoned, God hadn't been responsive to my prayers about Bill through the years. Since I felt I was essentially on my own, I decided to act like it as well.

I was trying not to be frustrated with God, but my anger resurfaced quickly after Bill convinced the pastor at Evangelical Bible Church (the church he now claimed he was regularly attending) to try to persuade me I couldn't leave him for a second time. At a brief meeting called by the EBC pastor, I heard a reprise of all of the same "God" arguments that allegedly required me to stay and forgive Bill, regardless of the circumstances. The pastor also performed a rather bizarre ritual. He asked me to cut some holes in a sheet of paper, telling me that the holes symbolically removed Frank from my life. Candidly, I wanted to use the scissors on the pastor's necktie.

Once again, Bill's surrogates were trying to guilt me back into our dysfunctional marriage. Not happening . . . not this time.

Frank and Divorce #2 from Bill
In March 1994, I left Bill for Frank. More accurately, I decided to divorce Bill, largely because I believed it was only a matter of time before the familiar pattern of his misconduct would repeat itself.

In preparing this *Janplan* exit, I made certain that my mother, sister, and a few close friends knew something about Bill's most recent misconduct. I needed some support. I wanted to share the information I had been keeping secret for years even if I would, once again, receive rolled eyes as a reaction. I did, and I did.

Of course, as I left my second marriage to Bill, I was again dragging a huge sled filled with guilt behind me. Once again, I had a fallen into a romance prior to my divorce. Again, Jan was exchanging a sin for a sin. Jan had also failed again in her ongoing codependent efforts to save her marriage and to be a model Christian wife.

My Sixteen-Day Marriage to Frank

Frank and I didn't go on a honeymoon. It wasn't important to me. After all, I didn't really think of Frank in a romantic way. He was a friend who knew both Bill and me. He knew about Bill's misconduct and he felt sorry for me. He was stable. Good enough foundation for a happy marriage, right?

Reprise my ill-fated twelve-day union with John. What was I thinking? Frank and I didn't have a physical attraction. Further, he wasn't a bit interested in ever sharing a spiritual connection or in joining a church. Was this union simply a product of "beware the woman scorned"?

Frank had essentially been a bachelor for the nine years he had been separated from his wife before we got together. He was very set in his ways. Dinner had to be on the table by 6:00 p.m. even if one of the kids had sports practice. He wasn't flexible or very friendly with the kids. There was no spark and I certainly should have realized that before accepting his proposal. Yet, I was so tired of the dysfunction and drama of life with Bill that I convinced myself that Frank's stability would somehow make up for the other deficits in our relationship.

The guilt over how I handled my most recent split from Bill was also eating me up. Frank knew what was going to happen before I told him. He knew I didn't love him. I think he even knew I was eventually going to go back to Bill . . . again.

Frank didn't deserve any heavenly retribution, even if I did. I was certain God's wrath was going to rain down as a result of this *Janplan*. The speeches from Bill, the Village Bible people, and the EBC pastor were again echoing in my head. "Marriage is forever. God gave us our kids. We were married in the church. Christians are to forgive others lest they not be forgiven. We belong together despite any challenges. It is a wife's duty to stay with her husband, regardless of his behavior or her feelings."

Frank didn't object to the divorce, nor did he raise any issues concerning the financial terms for extinguishing our marriage. Even if I never really loved Frank, I did respect and care for him. I was thankful for the way he handled my yo-yo decisions and the embarrassing circumstances of our brief marriage and our divorce.

"Quid Pro Quo" Family Dysfunction

Whenever I caught Bill committing one of his "serious" offenses, I typically demanded he perform several acts of repentance to atone for his behavior. I almost always told him that, if he failed to follow through, I would leave him. Within days, weeks, or at most a few months, the promises were always broken.

So, was I denied my quid pro quo each time Bill breached his promises of good behavior? After discovering his bad behavior, this codependent would briefly gain the upper hand. I could temporarily exert some control over his conduct and our relationship. I would issue some ultimatums to force Bill to shape up. In reality, however, I had learned from my dad, years earlier, that the lecture was more important than any real behavioral changes. Bill soon understood that as well, immediately resorting back to his pattern of bad behaviors, with little fear of any permanent negative consequences.

Still, in my mind at the time, my ultimatums made sense. I reasoned that Bill and I were working at establishing guidelines and boundaries critical to repairing our marriage. Query: Can you repair a marriage if the two people in the marriage don't respect and don't trust each other?

Regardless, that is how we codependents tend to handle things. It's more about the process than the solution. We are attracted to the turmoil we know. The familiarity breeds an odd, anxiety-filled sort of "comfort." We become addicted to the upset and uncertainty of a chaos-dominated household.

It's an adrenaline shot; we often exhibit physical symptoms (i.e., my neck tightness) that accompany the latest disruptive event. Of course, as codependents, we would vehemently deny any insinuation that we *need* or *enjoy* the adrenaline rush. Nonetheless, tumult is what we understand. We feel alive because we feel needed. We also have a false belief that we can fix the abuser who kick-starts the household drama which rapidly becomes our "normal."

Trying to make right my estranged relationship with Jesus wasn't even on my radar screen at this point. I was separated from my Creator. I was totally immersed in Jan's dysfunctional world, desperately trying to figure a way out on my own.

Over the years, in return for tolerating Bill's repeated acting out, the quid pro quo rewards I reaped were unilateral control over the checkbook, freedom to decorate the home as I desired, and the ability to travel and structure my friendships as I wanted.

Was I really willing to trade a dysfunctional, emotionless, uncommunicative, godless, intimacy-free marriage in return for spending authority and the right to go anywhere and do anything I wanted, just like he did? Of course, that was never part of my *Janville* dream. My fantasy was a secure, stable, loving Christian family. However, given Bill's misbehavior, my codependency, and my running from Jesus, I accepted this abnormal trade-off for years. In my mind, it still gave me a shot at my dream. By doing so, I inadvertently reinforced Bill's apparent belief that we had a marriage relationship in which both of us paid for, and got, just what we wanted.

Marriage #3: Back on the Not-So-Merry-Go-Round

I married Bill for a third time in May 1995.

As we jumped into marriage number three, Bill seemed to be trying to make it work. He came home at night. He agreed to my prohibitions against lying and sneaking around. He seemingly even acquiesced to my rule, "One beer and you're outta here."

Granted, his explosive, abusive anger and selfishness hadn't been eliminated, but most of my major objections were seemingly being addressed. As a result of the CCC scandal, however, regular church attendance was no longer consistently imposed as a mandatory requirement.

Another change as we headed into marriage number three, was me—specifically, how I was handling the past. I finally understood that I had to forgive Bill for his previous sins. I had to move forward or I would be moving backward. Forgiveness meant not bringing up his female friends as leverage in our third marriage. I had to put them behind us. I told Bill as much.

While I wasn't completely certain I could do it, I knew I had to try, or I would undermine marriage number three before it ever got off the ground. I would like to say that my deep, sustaining relationship with Jesus led me to this understanding, but that would be false. My faith was at low ebb. Still, my basic understanding of the Bible and human nature conjoined to lead me away from retribution and punishment.

By the time Bill and I tied the knot the third time, cell phone technology helped me sidestep some of his meltdowns. For example, whenever I cleaned the house, I got in the habit of taking cell photographs of his piles of stuff. If I needed to move things temporarily to dust, I could get everything back in the same location to comply with his "don't ever, ever touch my stuff" rule. After all, we codependents learn how to fix things (even if most of our fixes never really solve any of the underlying problems).

Choosing to Stand Up or Sit Down

Why didn't I ever really stand up against Bill's angry explosions? Why couldn't I stop his misconduct? Why didn't I stomp out during the first marriage and just keep on walking? For years, I couldn't really understand why Dad's tough girl was so weak in this area of her life.

There was no rational explanation I could offer my parents, sister, or friends that could help them understand why I would return to Bill for a third time. In fact, I couldn't even offer myself a real coherent explanation for my decision. However, in retrospect, now years later, I can see that the reasons I stuck around weren't all that complicated.

First, I needed a husband to live with me in *Janville*. I needed a father for my kids. *I was in love with my Janville dream of love.* I was also terrified Bill would leave us if I stood up for myself. The thought of making it in the world as a single mom, living on a retail associate or part-time aerobic instructor's salary, wasn't particularly inviting. I was scared to death of being on my own.

Second, I continued to hope that my prayers for a divinely inspired reformation of Bill's character might be answered by God. Even if those prayers weren't answered, perhaps my ongoing codependent efforts to figure out and fix the "Bill puzzle" would ultimately bring about the changes I craved. If God wasn't going to help solve Jan's problems, perhaps Jan could get it done herself.

Another reason for returning was that I wasn't sure what a *real* marriage should look like or how it should function. I had witnessed my mother's subservient role in a marriage that was fueled by anger and substance abuse. Perhaps what I had with Bill wasn't that far from "normal."

Fourth, I have always hated conflict. I can't stand tension at home. I want people to be happy. I love to laugh and to help others laugh. I want people to get along. I have always wanted to help solve others' problems so they can feel joy and happiness. I also didn't want the conflict that I knew the boys and I would experience if Bill and I tried to handle a joint custody arrangement.

I also didn't leave because emotional abuse is a large stick that can be used to control the abuse victim. My husband knew he could use my fear as his rope to pull me back. My codependent addiction, which I define as my lifelong desire to try to fix and control things, played right into his hand and his use of manipulation, fear, anger, and intimidation. He knew I wouldn't be quick to leave . . . I needed to try to fix the chaos. I was needed to solve the problems.

Finally, my guilty conscience, partially the result of my twisted understanding of Christian obedience, also helped act as a rubber band, rebounding me back to Bill. The Village Bible book of "thou shall not" rules told me that I needed to be a better, more submissive wife. God didn't want me to stand up. It was my duty to forgive and forget, regardless of the offense and circumstances. My belief that I had a duty to make Bill happy was a constant driving force in my life for decades. Even if God couldn't forgive me, somehow, I needed to forgive Bill. The Bible told me so, I thought.

Emotional abuse can intertwine in strange ways with unreasonable life expectations and a guilt-based religious faith. Bill understood that my marriage and family expectations, my personal insecurities, his questionable religious doctrine, and his temper could pull me back into the abused caretaker role that suited his needs. By using our family, my *Janville* dream, and the sacrament of marriage, Bill repetitively shamed me back into the relationship.

In retrospect, I can see how I also helped set the stage on which our dysfunctional marriage dramas played out. As early as our first few months of dating, I didn't confront Bill's anger, I didn't address his lies, I didn't demand accountability and respect. I let him set the ground rules in our relationship. Then I didn't realistically or firmly object when I found them unsatisfactory.

I didn't stand up because, as a codependent, I loved to be needed and I needed to be loved. Helping solve a problem for someone else means you are needed, right? Being needed should mean that people will like you—and even love you, ok? Satisfying others' needs gives you a purpose in life, doesn't it? And having a purpose gives life meaning? Good questions. Jan just provided bad answers.

"Vacation Bill": My Dream Husband

In *Janville,* I was married to a Bill I used to call "Vacation Bill." He was the husband and father who was relaxed, fun to be around, great with the kids and others, generally nice to me, and who didn't drink or explode in anger (sometimes). Even better, Vacation Bill actually existed in real life (sometimes).

I always believed that Bill had it in him. I wanted to believe that God, or Bill's codependent wife, could bring it to the surface. I refused to let go of my *Janville* dream that the considerate and friendly man I infrequently saw could become a permanent fixture in our home.

Vacation Bill could be thoughtful and interactive. When he coached baseball for our boys, the kids on the team and the other parents liked him. He related well to kids. He was encouraging and supportive.

When he taught our boys to fish, hunt, and ski, he also generally demonstrated a patience that was rarely evident in his other interactions with the boys. Bottom line, when Vacation Bill was doing something *he* wanted to do, something that mattered to *him*, he had the capacity to be warm and engaging.

This version of Bill appeared most frequently to the family or select friends while we were on vacation, fishing, or skiing—activities Bill loved. We have some photos and vacation memories that prove he was real. It was *this* Bill that I believed I could nurture, shame, or otherwise prod into existence on a regular basis, if I tried hard enough. I just needed to be good enough, persuasive enough, strong enough, competent enough, beautiful enough, supportive enough . . . you get the picture.

Unfortunately, I didn't understand, until after our third marriage ended, that I couldn't turn Bill into Vacation Bill permanently. Only he (and God) could make that change, and he didn't want to do it. He wanted to be the Bill that focused on Bill. He wanted to be the Bill that took advantage of, and intimidated, others when it suited his own purposes. He wanted what he wanted, when and how he wanted it.

Vacation Bill memories were the ones I glorified and clung to when I retreated to be with my dream family and dream husband in *Janville*. Those were the unrealistic desires and fleeting memories that brought me back into marriage with Bill three times. Unfortunately, those fleeting desires and memories were not my daily reality.

Life Compartments: My Key to Sanity

I was always good at compartmentalizing. A childhood spent with two alcoholic parents taught me how to put volatile family issues into an imaginary box, close the lid, and put it on the shelf. After all, if you're not going to communicate about a problem or make any real effort to change the behaviors that cause it, why waste any time worrying about it? Put it in the box. Pretend everything is normal . . . at least until someone or something jars the lid of the box open and the demons jump out.

I took the same approach in my marriages with Bill. Unless his behavior demanded immediate attention, I tried to store our unhappy, dysfunctional relationship in a fictitious box. I went on with the rest of the activities that brought some happiness to my life, including my gardening, shopping, girl friendships, school and sports activities with the boys, furniture refinishing, aerobics instruction, and so on. I wanted to stay happy, upbeat, and productive. That is what *Janville* needed to look like, at least from the outside.

The Girl Who Jumped into Bill's Truck...

By April 2000, still in marriage number three, Bill and I were largely back to our usual routines. He was fishing and working. I was taking care of the family and working. Our youngest, Sam, was really struggling with math at that time. He had a very important test coming up shortly, so I pressed Bill to help him.

Bill excelled at math in school, but he usually wasn't willing to help the boys with their math projects. He was easily frustrated, and the kids grew anxious if they weren't able to grasp the concepts quickly.

On this occasion, Bill agreed to take the time to help Sam after school at 3:45 p.m. so he would be ready for his math test the next day. However, like so many times in the past, the appointed time came and went. Bill didn't show. I was more upset than usual. This test was very important for Sam's education. Dad had promised to assist.

Around 7:30 p.m., the phone rang. I was simultaneously angry and relieved that it was my husband, but he quickly told me I wasn't going to be happy. I instantly assumed he had been in a car accident and frantically asked him where he was. When he replied, "Torrance . . . in jail and my car was impounded," my anger flashed, and I ran to the laundry room to finish the conversation.

"Were you in an accident? What happened?" I urgently inquired, as usual fearing the worst.

Bill said he was fine. Then he admitted to having had a "couple" of drinks. He said he was on his way home to help Sam when he stopped at a traffic light where a girl asked for a ride and then suddenly jumped into his truck, uninvited and only partially clothed. According to Bill, just as he was ready to order her out of his vehicle, the cops suddenly arrived, arrested both of them, and impounded his car.

During the course of this tale, the familiar tightness in my neck was returning. Totally apart from what he did, I was furious that his self-ishness also meant he wasn't around to help Sam with his test. After Bill asked if I would come bail him out of jail and pay to get his truck released, it may have taken me twenty seconds before I could respond. When I finally spoke, I exclaimed in a low but angry voice, "*I would absolutely leave you to rot in jail were it not for Sam's test.*"

I was in dangerous territory that evening. My mind was racing in *Janland.* How many other times had he sought such "friendship" without getting caught? Trying to control myself, I told Bill when he got home that he was going to work as long as necessary to help Sam finish studying for his test. I bailed him and his truck out. He bailed Sam out and our son passed his test. Just another happy family memory . . .

Bill's Retirement: His Free Time = My Full Time

Bill retired in 2005, ten years into our third marriage. For thirty-five years, Bill had typically worked twenty-four-hour shifts, but only on average about ten to fourteen days per month. That left the remaining days of each month for the pursuit of his personal interests. I never attempted to place restrictions on Bill's time off for a couple of reasons. Viscerally, I knew he lived for his hobbies, not me or what I wanted for our family. I also knew I would be starting an argument that I could never win.

When Bill retired, what would have normally been a joyous occasion for most couples proved to be a very ominous one for me. Before retirement, when Bill was at work, I knew he couldn't be getting in trouble. Now retired, he was going to have every day open for his personal pursuits. That would mean I would need to devote virtually all my time to monitoring his free time if I wanted to know what he was doing. I knew he had no intention of spending his free hours with me.

By 2005, Mark was working. Tommy was twenty-five and Sam was a senior in high school. However, I was still performing most of my "mom duties" as the older boys often lived at home to save money.

Grocery shopping, laundry, cleaning, and other duties still needed to be handled for all *four* of my boys. I needed to keep everyone happy . . . that's what I do.

My constant worrying about Bill's daily activities took much of the joy out of my daily activities. I was also angry with God because babysitting my husband was still one of my duties. After my mom had a stroke in 2009, I needed to be a temporary caregiver for her. I was happy to care for her. However, my husband was a physically and mentally competent fifty-plus-year-old adult. "God," I sometimes lamented, "why have I been burdened with the responsibility of also being my husband's caregiver for over three decades?"

Eventually, I started planning my daily activities around Bill's so I wouldn't be leaving him at home alone. If Bill was scheduled to be out of the house, I would also plan to run errands at the same time so I could be home when he returned. If he was supposed to be home, I wanted to be home as well so I would know if he was there.

During our third marriage, I even thought about purchasing a satellite vehicle tracker to help me keep up with his movements. Sadly, I was quite certain that the other wives in *Janville* were not using GPS technology to keep constant tabs on their husbands.

Chat Room Pop-Ups
In 2007, I was on our home computer checking sales at my favorite retailers when a pop-up appeared on the lower left of my screen with the note, "*Hi, Are you there?*" I responded, "*Who is this?*"

While awaiting a response, my neck was tightening, and my mind was off to *Janland* trying to figure out my husband's latest adventure. When the person didn't respond quickly, I sent another note: "*I'm Bill's wife, who is this?*" No response, but now I was determined to find the source of the message. I soon discovered a series of emails between my husband and at least fourteen women. While none of the communications were overtly sexual, it was clear that Bill was chatting with females and attempting to arrange meetings with several of them.

In particular, one set of emails was with a woman he had tried to meet recently. Her last note to Bill stated that, unfortunately, she had to cancel their scheduled meeting because she needed to accompany her daughter on a school field trip to a small marine museum in Laguna Beach. After her trip, Bill had written her the following note: *"I went to the museum just so I could see you. I hid behind a pole, but I was staring at you wishing that I could give you a hug."*

The familiar tightness in my neck was extremely uncomfortable by this time. Knowing that he would deny these emails and then immediately delete them if I confronted him, I decided I needed to make copies.

When Bill came home, I asked him about the pop-ups and his chat room activities. As expected, he immediately stonewalled. When I told him I had copies of his communications with the women, including the "hug" lady, he immediately moved from defense to offense. He flew into a tirade of anger, accusing me of spying on him. After a couple of minutes he suddenly did an about-face, attempting to sidestep the issue by claiming that it "didn't mean anything since I never met any of those women," and "it was just a game, *something that people do.*"

I recall exhaling a huge sigh of relief. I was so happy that his extensive, secret chat activities with fourteen different women and his approximately three-hour round-trip drive to Laguna Beach to stand behind a pole to tell a woman he wanted to hug her could not be understood as an attempt to "hook up" with other females. As always, his innovative explanations and excuses set my mind at ease. After all, as Bill had explained, "it's just something that people do."??!??

The Girl in the Prescription Bottle

On November 14, 2008, our son Tommy got married. It was a peak *Janville* life moment and memory for me. I witnessed a wedding ceremony celebrating love while surrounded by my entire family and many of our closest friends. Less than a week later, however, another *Janville* mountaintop quickly turned into another *Janland* valley.

On November 20, 2008, Bill came home later than usual, plunked himself into his recliner, and fell fast asleep. About fifteen minutes later, he was snoring soundly when his cell phone rang from the small basket he kept near the chair. I ran to turn it off, knowing that if the ring woke him up he would likely be in a bad mood—one that would later become my fault.

As I grabbed for the jingling phone, I inadvertently knocked the basket, and everything tumbled to the floor. Panicked that Bill might wake and discover my clumsiness, I was quickly scooping the contents of the basket from the floor when I noticed a partially empty prescription bottle with a piece of paper inside it. After carefully replacing the other items in the basket, I opened the bottle and found a woman's name (Phyllis) and phone number written on the Costco receipt. After Bill awoke from his afternoon siesta, I inquired about the woman's name and number.

As expected, Bill lit into me. "What are you doing, going through my stuff? Haven't I told you to leave my things alone? You have no right to be searching through my things trying to find something you can use against me." Blah, blah.

After weathering the first wave of vitriolic anger, I asked again about the woman named Phyllis. Bill claimed the name and phone number were from a woman who had offered to do some painting on one of my mother's rental properties years earlier. When I pointed out that the woman's name was on a Costco receipt dated November 18, a mere four days after Tommy's wedding, he swallowed and quickly reversed course.

Now he defended himself by saying that he was standing in the Costco pharmacy checkout line when this woman just handed him a paper with her name and phone number. I erupted, tossing a rare profanity at him to emphasize my disgust. Bill dismissively laughed at me, sneering, "Great, I like to see you like that. If you had been more like that during our marriages, perhaps I would have come home and not done some of the things I did."

I was incredulous. Really? Talk about turning the tables . . . now I'm being blamed for his lying, drinking, and other bad behaviors because I wasn't mean and nasty enough to keep him in line? Bill had indeed done away with *PollyJana*. The woman who had taken her place in this marriage was far less kind and, by that time, far less connected to God.

The Death of *PollyJana*: Hating the Person I'd Become
Spending decades in an emotionally or physically abusive relationship can actually rewire your brain. It can transform you in ways you would have never contemplated. It can even change you into a person you might eventually learn to hate.

When I met Bill in the spring of 1970, I was immature, quite naive, and very trusting. *PollyJana* was a happy blond who wanted to be everyone's friend, the person who wanted to believe in the good in everyone. Quick to smile and laugh, I was optimistic. I worked to make people happy. My sense of humor and my desire to please others made me accessible and fun to be around.

By 1990, *PollyJana* had become a different person. I was no longer nearly as naive, trusting, and optimistic, nor as willing to believe in everyone. While I was still quick to smile and laugh, the world was no longer the sunny *Janville* place of my dreams. Bill's bad behaviors, my reactions, and the chaos, drama, and uncertainty that constantly swirled in my life had changed me.

Where had *PollyJana* gone? What had I become? While I still tried to act like "nice and happy Jan" in front of the boys, my friends, and coworkers, I was not that person with Bill—nor was I that person on the inside. At home, I cried frequently. I was short and often abrupt with Bill. I was estranged from my relationship with Jesus.

In the final years of our last marriage, I would pray frequently at night that Bill would quit breathing. Then I would immediately pray a second prayer to ask forgiveness for my first prayer. To be blunt, during the last three of years of our third marriage, I hated Bill. I also hated parts of myself.

This "new" Jan was more suspicious, more negative, quick to anger, more reactive . . . not the person God made me to be. I had turned into an enabler/forensic investigator. I still tended to enable some of Bill's misconduct because I didn't want to deal with his abusive, angry reactions. I never set and enforced boundaries in our relationship. At the same time, I had turned into a kind of CSI investigator to discover the very misconduct I often helped facilitate.

I hated my investigator role but, in my mind, I only had two options: try to investigate and confront Bill about his misconduct in the hope that he would change, or simply let things go and give up on my *Janville* dream. In reality, I should have recognized that the dream had been lost years earlier.

Bill figured out, early in our first marriage, that Jan wasn't going to follow through on her threats. Bill also figured out alternative avenues to have his way and his fun, despite the occasional burden of some temporary "sanctions" at home. After retirement, since he was now more tethered to home, Bill also figured out that the Internet could take him places he wanted to go without ever leaving the house.

Porn Again, Not Born Again

Late in our third marriage, the Internet, with its voluminous online porn sites and hook-up chat rooms, made Bill's "networking" connections easier. On several occasions, I discovered Bill using our home computer to view online porn. When he was confronted, he used excuses and his volatile anger to back me down.

"It just popped up when I was searching the web for fishing lures."

"What are you doing, spying on me again?" and on and on.

One morning in 2013, I hopped on my stationary bike in the garage at 8:30 a.m. for my usual hour of exercise. I had inadvertently left my water bottle inside, so I jumped off and opened the side door into the house. I could see into our home office from the side garage door. Bill was on the computer, but he rapidly closed out a screen once the garage door opened, quickly turning to me to ask what I was doing. Telling him I forgot my water bottle, I asked him what he was doing. Looking a bit sheepish, he replied that he had just been checking the weather reports to decide when to go fishing.

I grabbed my water and headed back out to the garage. However, instead of jumping back on my bike, I decided to wait a few minutes and then do a recheck on Bill. The look on his face told me he was up to something—I decided to find out what it was. After a couple of minutes, I quietly snuck out the back door of the garage, got on my hands and knees and started to crawl to the office window on the side of the house.

As I was slinking along the ground, the sheer ridiculousness of this part of my life came crashing in on me. After essentially tolerating years of lies and other serious marital offenses, now I was surreptitiously inching my way along the ground to spy on my husband to see whether he was watching porn on the family computer. I was quite sure that the Bible's definition of love in 1 Corinthians 13 didn't include this type of husband–wife interaction.

Reaching the study window, I cautiously elevated and peered in. Bill was enjoying an interactive video chat . . . with a woman who was entertaining herself, and him, with a feather. Outraged, I banged several times loudly on the window. Then I jumped up and ran quickly to the street with Bill in hot pursuit, shouting his usual cadre of excuses and hollow apologies.

It seemed that nothing was going to change this guy—not threats, prayers, pleading, tears, humiliation, forced church attendance, grounding . . . nothing. It was at this moment that I decided it was time for Jan to start looking out for herself.

Trying to Buy Happiness

During the nineteen years of my third marriage to Bill, I focused on keeping busy. I had the boys, my friends, my caretaker duties, and my hobbies. Each day was a whirlwind of activity. In my mind, my busyness established my worthiness. While I still occasionally thought about God and missed being in relationship with Him, I had given up on trying to drag my family to church. I think I also subconsciously rationalized that our busy family activities provided an excuse for my decision to run away from Jesus.

After my mom had her stroke in 2009, I discovered yet another common path many of us pursue to try to find happiness and contentment in this world. Money from my mother's estate paid off family bills and provided me with money for trips, shopping, and the boys. Candidly, at this point in my life, I felt I deserved it. Since I couldn't seem find happiness in my marriage, at least for a short time, I believed that money would provide it.

> No one can serve two masters. For you will hate one and love the other; you will be devoted to one and despise the other. You cannot serve God and be enslaved to money.
> —Matthew 6:24 NLT

Mom's real estate career took off after she and Dad were divorced during my senior year of high school. Mom purchased rental homes and she did well in the stock market. Her financial numbers, scrawled on anything flat, filled boxes in her home. Her money was far more important to her than her family. She had few friends. She eventually died as a wealthy woman in 2011. There was no point in having a memorial service . . . no one would have come.

Six months after their divorce, Dad accepted a two-year severance/early retirement package from his company. He moved to Florida where he spent his retirement fishing and playing golf. His later years were plagued with health problems, many of which could be attributed to his long history of heavy drinking and smoking. Dad took his own life in 2000.

When Mom passed away, she left all of her assets to my sister and me. We divided her estate equally. Between 2009–2012, we spent some on ourselves but gave most of her money to our now-grown kids by gifting them homes, cars, and cash. Her money was the only gift Mom ever offered her grandkids; unfortunately, they did not receive the gift of her time or her love.

Beth or I never wanted Mom or Dad's money. All we ever wanted from our parents was a stable, loving home environment—the one thing they couldn't give us. That's why my fantasy home in *Janville,* filled with happiness, stability, and Christ's presence, was the gift I was most determined to offer to my kids.

Unfortunately, although Bill and I didn't move constantly, the perpetual chaos, anger, and turmoil in our home denied my boys the *Janville* environment I so wanted to provide. As I later realized, the gift of Mom's money turned out to be a poor substitute.

Filling the Void with Small-g Gods

Our family had a number of dogs through the years. If one of them had a sore paw, I observed they would usually do two things: (1) rely primarily upon their other three legs for mobility, and (2) tough it out, often acting as though nothing was seriously wrong. Over the years of my difficult marriages to Bill, I realized that I had learned a lesson from my pets: adapt as necessary and tough it out. Figure out how to fill your loneliness void. Try not to show your hurt. Fake happy.

To survive, I latched on to several small-*g* gods to whom I offered my attention and my allegiance. Like many of us, rather than returning in prayer, with a contrite heart, to the real God of the universe, I used worldly coping strategies (i.e., my *Janplans*) to try to survive.

Frenetic activity has always been my primary adaptation technique. It is an approach that was even recommended by a counselor, years earlier, so I wouldn't become depressed about my marriage. Of course, for years, much of my busyness was centered around rearing children.

I spent hundreds of hours volunteering at the boy's schools. I represented the high school baseball program on the Athletic Boosters Board, graded papers for teachers, worked as a room mother, soccer referee and coordinator, and baseball scorekeeper. I baked dozens of treats for teacher appreciation, helped as a team mom for baseball, soccer, and basketball, drove hundreds of carpools, and engaged in a myriad of other school-related tasks for my kids. And because I had three boys scattered thirteen years apart, I was involved in their respective school activities for twenty-seven years.

Still, I can see now that the busyness that constantly filled my days also became a small-*g* god I worshipped. My "Super Mom" badge, awarded to Jan by Jan, worn proudly as a symbol of my self-worth, also served as a makeshift Band-Aid to cover the wound that surrounded my emptiness. Of course, when we fill every waking moment with busyness and activities, we can't fill those moments with self-reflection, counseling, or time with Jesus.

> Here I am! I stand at the door and knock. If anyone
> hears my voice and opens the door, I will come in . . .
> —Revelation 3:20 NIV

> Truly my soul finds rest in God; my salvation comes
> from him.
> —Psalm 62:1 NIV

Another small-*g* god for me has been shopping. I have been a shopper my entire life. In reality, I love the quest far more than the conquest. I love finding the bargain and the good buy. I can easily walk away from an overpriced item but I will walk miles searching for an underpriced one.

I have also had a lifelong love affair with clothes. I can be tough, but I'm also a "girly" girl. I want to look pretty. At the apex of my shopping addiction, I had walk-in closet the size of a bedroom that included a sitting area and a full makeup vanity and sink. I can see now, in retrospect, that trying to decorate myself on the outside could never make me more beautiful on the inside.

> And I want women to be modest in their appearance.
> They should wear decent and appropriate clothing and

not draw attention to themselves by the way they fix
their hair or by wearing gold or pearls or expensive
clothes. For women who claim to be devoted to God
should make themselves attractive by the good things
they do.
—1 Timothy 2:9–10 NLT

You shall have no other gods before me.
—Exodus 20:3 NIV

Your beauty should not come from outward adorn-
ment, such as elaborate hairstyles and the wearing of
gold jewelry or fine clothes. Rather, it should be that
of your inner self, the unfading beauty of a gentle and
quiet spirit, which is of great worth in God's sight.
—1 Peter 3:3–4 NIV

As a codependent and a person who has struggled with low self-
esteem, I spent much of my life working to please others and to solve
problems for them. I hoped that other people would think well of me,
that they would like me. Now I understand that part of my motivation
for helping and problem solving was really a selfish one—the very one
Jesus warns us against—the quid pro quo. My need to be needed and my
need to be loved often added *self* into what should have otherwise been
selfless acts of love.

What is done *out of love* should not be done *for love*. The Bible tells
us that love is not jealous and it does not demand its own way. While
we are instructed by the Bible to "love your neighbor," Jesus didn't instruct us to sell our love or to pay others for their love. For years, I
didn't fully understand the distinction between offering unconditional
love to someone and working to please others so they will like you or
recognize you, or so you can feel good about yourself. Huge difference.

Searching for "Vacation Bill" One Final Time: Our 2014 UK Trip

I have always loved traveling abroad. I have traveled to Europe at least eight times, including four trips to the United Kingdom. I fell in love with England . . . the country, its history, its people, and the laid-back tempo of life in the English countryside.

One of those trips to England occurred in August 2014. It was spawned by a wonderful idea I had to save our third marriage. Why not take a four-week vacation with my husband to England, I thought? I persuaded Bill to go with me. I hoped the August trip might bring out Vacation Bill, that guy who had infrequently demonstrated he could enjoy, and even be enjoyable, while away from home. Who knows, I thought, perhaps Bill and I would finally feel that spark I so longed for in our marriage.

Unfortunately, the trip was a complete, unmitigated disaster. Bill complained from the moment the plane took off until the return flight landed. He hated the busyness of London, walking to historic sites, the tour group we were with, the food, the accommodations . . . you name it. Since I had planned the entire trip, I was the cause of his unhappiness, of course. I was the person to blame for having wasted a month of his life.

Bill's dissatisfaction was so visible that our tour driver and other members of the tour group eventually started to make jokes about "Mr. Grumpy." While I was initially embarrassed, I quickly decided that I wasn't going to let Bill ruin my trip. I started spending more time with the other guests and our bus driver, Sean.

Sean was funny. Bald, missing a tooth, nearly as round as he was tall, he worked to involve his guests in the adventure of the tour. He engaged with everyone. Since I am a talker, Sean and I hit it off immediately, joking and talking both individually and as part of the group. Meanwhile Mr. Grumpy pouted in the back of the bus, in the line to the museum, or in the corner of the restaurant.

Time spent with Bill was unbearable, but Sean helped me enjoy the trip despite my husband's bad behavior. Bill didn't like Sean. To Bill, Sean was a mere servant, a bus driver. He had nothing to offer Bill. Also,

Bill didn't like the attention Sean was showing me. Subconsciously, I probably enjoyed the fact that Bill was a bit irritated.

At the end of the trip, Sean and I exchanged phone numbers, email addresses, and Facebook connections. I did so with some of the other tour guests as well, though I can't say I had any intention of really keeping up with anyone. However, when Bill came home staggering again the following month, I connected with Sean via Facebook Messenger to give him an update. I had no one in the States who would listen to my latest "Bill's Bad Behavior Story"; my friends and family had given up on this topic years earlier.

Beginning to *Janplan* My Final Exit
In mid-September 2014, another drinking episode set in motion a chain of events that pointed us toward the finish line for our final marriage. One evening, I stayed at my sister's house in Garden Grove. Before driving to my sister's, I had asked Bill to make sure he was home that night because he needed to feed the dog while I was gone. When I quizzed him the next day about his activities the previous evening, my neck was tight. I already had independent evidence that he had been out and hadn't come home to feed our pet.

In response to my questions, Bill erupted like a geyser. "I'm so sick and tired of you always asking where I went and who I was with," he exclaimed. "Let me tell you where we are at this point. You got a choice: you can go with Plan A or Plan B. Under Plan A, we can stay married but you back off all your questions, I don't go to church, and, in the future, you don't ask me where I have been or what I've been doing . . . I'm done putting up with it. I'll do what I want, when I want to do it. With Plan B, you continue your questions and investigations, and we get a divorce."

When I asked again where he had been the previous evening, Bill turned on his heel and yelled, "Plan B it is." Then he opened the door to the house and shouted at Sam, "Your mom and I are splitting up."

I was in a state of shock at that moment, trying to understand his twisted logic. He's asking for a divorce now because he didn't come home last night and he won't let me ask questions about it, I thought. Really?

At the time, I didn't think Bill meant what he was saying. He was probably trying to call my bluff, assuming I wouldn't consider Plan B. If I chose Plan A, he could do anything he wanted in the future . . . no restrictions, no accountability, no investigations or repercussions for his conduct. However, when Bill refused to change his position on the divorce the following day, I became upset. This guy is going to divorce me because he lied, again, and he violated his no-drinking promise, again? I was floored. I had expected to be in control of the timing of any final divorce.

I decided to set up a meeting with a counselor to discuss Bill's ultimatum. The counselor somehow managed to listen to my tearful forty-minute summary of our dysfunctional and dramatic four decades of marital history with a blank face. She then advised that we should consider a cooling-off period. She also urged us to consider some couples counseling. Imagine that . . .

When I informed Bill what the counselor said, he sneered that he had no interest in going to see a "shrink." However, he also told me that he didn't think we needed to get a divorce, though he made no effort to apologize for his earlier threats. He was steadfast in his declaration that he would never go for any counseling to address his misconduct or the problems in our relationship.

On October 12, 2014, Bill came home drunk again. On October 22, 2014, I filed for divorce for the third and final time.

The most recent drinking incidents and his ultimatums finally jarred me completely out of my *Janville* dream. Bill was going to keep drinking and he was going to keep lying about it. I finally came to the realization that I just couldn't continue pretending that this marriage was going to be any different from the preceding ones. It wasn't *if* it was going to end but rather *when and how* it would end.

Still, despite my mental and emotional exhaustion, I wasn't looking forward to cutting the cord on our marriage at this point. I had a sense that a final divorce might radically change the dynamics of our family, including my relationships with the boys. I knew Bill would claim victim status if I made the decision to end the marriage. After all, that was his MO in the past: abuse our relationship until I ran and then claim he was the victim of an unfaithful spouse.

I also knew he would use his bitterness toward me and his sporting relationships with the boys to try to commandeer their allegiance post-divorce. The male bond he shared with the boys through their mutual hobbies of fishing and hunting would be a powerful draw to keep the kids close to him.

On the bright side, at least at this point the boys were grown men, I reasoned. They had all received healthy distributions of my mother's money. Fortunately, I didn't need to fill the role of mommy and worry about their futures the way I did at the time of the first two divorces. I decided I had to hope that I could maintain my relationships with my boys even if I wasn't with their dad.

After I filed for our third divorce, Bill started referring to me as "the quitter." Knowing that I had stayed in our dysfunctional relationship for decades longer than I probably should have, Bill also knew how much the "quitter" label would irritate me. I was the tough girl who didn't quit. More emotional abuse in an effort to guilt me into staying. This time, however, I was determined to make the break once and for all.

I sent a one liner to Sean, the tour bus driver in England, letting him know that Mr. Grumpy had asked for a divorce. My note triggered a series of messages and emails that eventually lead to some lengthy phone conversations. Since I had fantasized about living in England, Sean's suggestion that I return for a visit helped fuel the ultimate *Janplan*.

The Craziest *Janplan*: Did the Devil Make Me Do It?
The craziest *Janplan* ever? In May 2015, I left my husband, family, and over four decades of my life in Los Angeles and moved across the ocean to live in Dover, Kent County, England.

Did I move to England for a fresh start? Certainly. Did I intend to live in England for the rest of my life? Yes. Did I want to divorce Bill once and for all, permanently severing the rubber band that brought us back together on three occasions? Definitely.

Did I move to England for another man? Not really. Was I trying to run away from my former life? I guess. Did I meet Sean and spend time with him? I did. Did I ever intend to marry Sean? No, but I was clearly starved for some attention.

Was I in relationship with God at this point? No, though I still prayed occasionally. However, my prayers weren't expressions of gratitude or prayers of humility. I did not ask Him for His plans for me, nor did I request His guidance and direction. Before moving to England, I essentially challenged Jesus, "Stop my move if you don't approve."

Did Christ respond to my prayers? Actually, I can see now that He did. Jesus released me to my latest *Janplan*, including whatever consequences were to flow from it. He knew I was going to pursue my plan anyway, regardless of my infrequent efforts to check in to offer Him meaningless veto power over my decision.

Did the devil make me do it? While the Evil One was undoubtedly excited about my new *Janplan*, I can't give him all the credit. Satan always needs a willing partner. He knew he had one. He didn't have to pull very hard at his end of the stick.

Seeking God's Stamp of Approval

Jesus knew that any prayers I was offering at this time weren't completely sincere. They weren't offered with an open and receptive heart. He knew I was just looking for an omnipotent stamp of approval for my England *Janplan*.

Think about it . . . one of the greatest mysteries of Christianity is how the omniscient, omnipresent, omnipotent God of the universe is content to wait for us to decide if we want a relationship with Him. We have free will. We get to determine if we want to embrace our Creator.

Jesus constantly pursues us in love. He wants to be in relationship with us. He offers us the truth that will set us free. But it is up to each one of us to decide to knock on the door He is waiting to open for us. If we don't want His peace, His grace, and His love, Christ allows us to reap the booby prizes offered by the small-*g* gods of this world that we choose to worship.

Let me be clear about one thing: even as I implemented my "ultimate" *Janplan,* I still believed that Jesus was my Lord. He is the Messiah who came to the world in human form to die for my death and my sins so that I might have eternal life through Him. I remained a believer—I just wanted to do things my way. I just wanted to call on Him for a little help, if necessary, as I followed my own path.

In reality, by this time in my life, I had strayed far away from the path of "selfless follower" and taken my own path of "selfish leader." God let me follow my own dead-end roadmap, even as His heart grieved over my decisions.

> Do nothing out of selfish ambition or vain conceit. Rather, in humility value others above yourselves, not looking to your own interests but each of you to the interests of the others.
> —Philippians 2:3–4 NIV

> And without faith it is impossible to please God, because anyone who comes to him must believe that he exists and that he rewards those who earnestly seek him.
> —Hebrews 11:6 NIV

The Quest: Searching for Jan in All the Wrong Places
By November 2014, I had convinced myself that I needed to walk away from family and friends that seemed to demand my love, my time, and my effort without offering me the same gifts in return. Rightly or wrongly, I felt underappreciated and overextended. Jan had convinced herself that she needed to find Jan. She had earned the right to be happy and she was going to find her happiness.

Thus was hatched the ultimate *Janplan*. I would show Bill. I would not only leave my family, my community, and my comfort zone but I would move to a foreign country. I might even date an overweight, balding bus driver with bad teeth and few financial resources. I would discover the real Jan and I didn't need anybody's help to do it. This tough girl could do it on her own.

Jan, the International Ping-Pong Ball

Between January 2015 and August 2015, I made five round trips between London and Los Angeles.

I visited England in January, hung out with Sean, and scouted for houses in Dover. I went back in March to visit again and made an offer on a lovely little cottage within miles of the Dover Castle and the White Cliffs. I returned to complete the home purchase in May 2015; in June I unloaded my shipping container of furniture and proceeded to try to establish my new home and life in Kent County.

Following a mid-June trip back to the USA to help my oldest son with some childcare responsibilities, I returned to England and stayed until August. Then I moved back to America permanently, followed by the return of my furniture in November 2015.

After spending a total of just eight weeks actually living abroad, *Janplan*: England was done.

Was my escape-to-England plan simply the craziest life decision this poor life decision-maker has ever made? Clearly. Was the plan impetuous and ill-considered? Yes. A financial disaster? Absolutely. A predictably horrendous decision that served to alienate my family and friends? Yes. The worst event in my entire life? Actually, no.

You see, God allows us to experience trials and tribulations in our lives. Our hardships may be the consequence of our own poor decisions (i.e., my escape to England) or they may simply be the product of our circumstances, a result of the broken world in which we live. Still, our life challenges can help us build perseverance and character. In fact, Jesus often uses our hardships to mold and shape us, to help us understand how much we need a spiritual relationship with Him and that we can depend on Him to help us through our trials.

> And we know that for those who love God all things work together for good, for those who are called according to his purpose.
> —Romans 8:28 ESV

> We also glory in our sufferings, because we know that suffering produces perseverance; perseverance, character; and character, hope.
> —Romans 5:3–4 NIV

> And God is faithful; he will not let you be tempted beyond what you can bear.
> —1 Corinthians 10:13 NIV

Rediscovering My Faith and My Family

I have never been as good a listener as I am a talker. And if, as the Bible says, God sometimes speaks in a still, small voice, I'm certain I have literally drowned Him out on multiple occasions with all my words, thoughts, and plans. Still, while my UK move was an extremely poor decision, I'm convinced God used it to speak to me—to open my ears, my eyes, and my heart to His love, His grace, and His plan for me. In fact, He used my ultimate *Janplan* to teach me lessons that have literally transformed my life. Here's how we get to the simple conclusion of my story . . .

Searching for a Rock—Not Another Man
As ill-considered as my England move proved to be, there was something about the finality of leaving America and purchasing a home in a foreign country that helped me understand that Jan needed to have a life apart from Bill. At the same time, I think I was also starting to comprehend that I needed a foundation for my life, an anchor that was more solid than my elusive childhood dream of *Janville*.

I didn't go to Kent County to substitute one husband for another. I hardly knew Sean. I spent less than one month of total time dating him before I returned to the US in August 2015. True, Sean could be funny and entertaining. However, I also discovered very quickly that he was not really committed to his professed Catholic faith and he was a heavy drinker with significant anger and male chauvinist control issues. Talk about potentially jumping from the frying pan into the fire. I certainly wasn't looking for another Bill, only with an English accent.

By the time I left for England, it was becoming clear to me that I needed to learn to stand on my own. My kids were grown now. During my entire adult life, I had always had a man to lean on. Jan needed to figure out who she was and what she needed in order to figure out how to fill that empty hole in her life.

Also, it was starting to dawn on me that, unless I learned to accept myself and overcome my codependent characteristics, I would probably never be able to love someone as part of a healthy partnership. The English countryside near the Straits of Dover, with its quiet hills and valleys, gave me the setting and the silence to start to chew on some of these issues.

The beauty and solitude of my life in Dover gave me time to communicate with Jesus. No, I hadn't jumped back into my prayer life with any real commitment by the first part of 2015. Still, I was thankful for God's protection as I relocated to England. I wasn't pretending that Christ was supportive of this *Janplan*. However, I was starting to believe that perhaps it wasn't God's plan that I return to an emotionally abusive, dysfunctional relationship with Bill yet another time.

My Bible studies and my fundamental Christian education impressed upon me that it is God's will that marriage should be a lifetime commitment. On that point even Bill, with his twisted, alt-interpretations of Scripture, was correct. However, I was also starting to believe that it may not be God's will that a marriage endures where one person suffers extreme emotional or physical abuse at the hands of the other.

Love is patient, love is kind . . . It does not dishonor others . . . it is not easily angered . . . Love does not delight in evil but rejoices with the truth. It always protects, always trusts . . .

—1 Corinthians 13:4–7 NIV

My Epiphany: Rain, Hail, and Jesus Washed Me Clean

England is a beautiful country filled with kind people. My neighbors in Dover, Mac and Kera, were wonderful folks and they remain close friends. My decision to leave England only eight weeks after I moved there had nothing to do with the England or its people; it had everything to do with God opening my eyes to His grace and His purpose for my life.

Between May 4 and June 12, 2015, I was busy unpacking—trying to turn my new house into a home. Though I have worked outside the home most of my life, my role in my *Janville* dream was that of wife, mother, and homemaker.

My home has always been important to me. Frankly, after leaving my family and friends in America, my house was all I had in England, especially since I discovered shortly after arriving that I would have some problems getting a work permit. (Ouch, should have checked out that issue before making this *Janplan*.) Nonetheless, I did what I always do when presented with a challenge: I dug in and tried to the make the best of things. I was going to make my little cottage home in the countryside as warm and inviting as possible.

Kent County is known as the "Garden of England" for its abundance of orchards and hops gardens. Some of its distinctively shaped, hops-drying buildings, known as oasts, have actually been converted into homes. Since I have always had a green thumb and I love to garden, Dover seemed to be an ideal location for my new life.

I bought my new home at a bargain price, particularly given the bonus of the lovely greenhouse that was situated in its side yard. After moving in, I decided to convert a dormant water fountain in the middle of my front yard into a lovely flower garden. I was exhilarated about trying to grow terraced floral arrangements in the fountain tiers. I bought dozens of beautiful flowers from the local nursery and looked forward to my planting day with anticipation.

On June 12, 2015, a warm morning sun rose in a cloudless blue sky, accompanied by a tiny breeze . . . a perfect day for gardening. About mid-morning, I excitedly gathered my plants around the fountain, dumped in my topsoil, and begin planting my new flowers.

Suddenly, within a matter of minutes, the sky clouded up and a strong breeze begin to blow. As I was deciding whether to postpone my planting, the horizon rapidly darkened. Instantly, the few raindrops that had begun to fall were transformed into coin-sized hail stones, painfully pelting me and my flowers. Out of nowhere, the strong breeze then transitioned into thirty-mile-per-hour gusts and the temperature began to plummet.

The flowers I had just planted were instantly ripped from their fragile moorings in the soil and were sent blowing like pinwheels down the driveway. Feeling the sting of the hail stones, I dashed down the drive after my precious flowers, most of which were moving far faster than I was. Flustered, wet, and sore, I gathered up the few I could catch, tossed them into my garden wagon along with my unplanted brood, and ran, sobbing and dragging the heavy wagon, toward my small greenhouse.

Once inside, I sat gushing tears, frustrated with the demise of my fountain planting, angry with the abrupt hailstorm. Suddenly, I heard a quiet voice in my head say, "*You don't belong here.*" Certain that I was just imagining things, I pushed my mind back to my gardening problems. A short time later, I again heard the voice say, "*This is not where you belong.*" The second time there was no mistaking that I had heard the voice clearly and distinctly. Yet, I was all by myself in my greenhouse, crying, cold, wet, and shaking. Where did this declaration come from? What did it mean?

I was determined to stick to my England decision. The stakes at play in this *Janplan* were high from any perspective—family, social, spiritual, and financial. I had to be Dad's tough girl. I had to get things under control . . . I had to belong here . . . Jan *had* to make this plan work.

> When pride comes, then comes disgrace, but with humility comes wisdom.
> —Proverbs 11:2 NIV

Suddenly, as quickly as they had started, the hail, wind, and rain outside the greenhouse stopped. Blue sky returned. The sun was shining brightly again. I opened the door and trudged back toward the fountain, dragging my planting wagon.

However, despite the sunlight, my heart was dark and heavy. My tears continued to flow intermittently all afternoon as I worked to complete my flower planting. I couldn't understand my sobbing . . . the sun was shining again, and I was back to gardening, my favorite hobby. Why was I blubbering? Inside, I felt broken, hollow, and completely sapped of energy.

Why am I struggling? I thought. Afterall, I was finally pursuing my *Janplan* without any interference from God, a husband, or family and friends that didn't always act and react as I wanted. I had broken away from years of a tortured relationship. I had some financial resources, my health, a beautiful home in a beautiful country, the freedom to do anything I pleased. I was finally living the dream . . . yet my tears were watering my newly planted flowers as I hovered over them.

Late in the afternoon, it hit me. In an instant, I realized that the tears I had been crying for hours were tears of shame and embarrassment. It was as though the hail that pelted my head had also pounded some sense into my confused brain. It was God who had been talking to me. And there was no parsing His message. The voice in my head was the Father telling His prodigal daughter to go home.

> Rejoice with me; I have found my lost sheep . . . There
> will be more rejoicing in heaven over one sinner who

repents than over ninety-nine righteous persons who
do not need to repent.
—Luke 15:6–7 NIV

"For this son of mine was dead and is alive again; he
was lost and is found." So they began to celebrate.
—Luke 15:24 NIV

How could I have been so blind and stupid? I suddenly realized that
no matter how many flowers I planted, I could never make this country
cottage in England my home. My family and friends were not here. I
couldn't simply run away from my mistakes by flying across the ocean.
Most importantly, I couldn't hide from God.

Where can I flee from your presence? If I go up to the
heavens, you are there; if I make my bed in the depths,
you are there.
—Psalm 139:7–8 NIV

Nothing in all creation is hidden from God's sight. Everything is uncovered and laid bare before the eyes of
him to whom we must give account.
—Hebrews 4:13 NIV

Over the years, I had allowed my pride and my selfish expectations to
replace God at the center of my life. I had convinced myself that achiev-
ing my *Janville* dream—my "princess fantasy" of a perfect marriage and
perfect family—would satisfy all of my needs. It hadn't worked. All my
Janplans had failed and they were destined to fail. Instantly, I realized
that I needed to look away from myself and to look up to God. It was
time to fix my eyes on Jesus, not on my reflection in the mirror. My
pride had become my God.

Fix your thoughts on Jesus.
                    —Hebrews 3:1 NIV

Do nothing out of selfish ambition or vain conceit.
                    —Philippians 2:3 NIV

The fatigue and brokenness I felt during my flower planting made sense now. My move to the UK wasn't a victory of freedom—it was a failure of bondage. I had been so tied up in my unrealistic life dream that when I couldn't make it happen, I had given up hope. I had decided I needed to escape my life because I was mentally, emotionally, physically drained by it.

Living life based upon what you feel you are entitled to is exhausting. Because we live in a broken world, you are setting yourself up for constant disappointment and disillusionment. Of course, it was easy for me to blame God when I didn't get what I wanted, when I wanted it. Like many of us, I wanted to blame someone else for my problems.

Of course, we all have emotionally-driven life fantasies, but we don't need to try to make them real. The Bible doesn't promise us a life filled with fulfilled dreams and earthly happiness. To the contrary, just as Jesus was tested during his forty days in the wilderness, we are also tested in a world that can be harsh and unforgiving. It's easy to have faith when everything is going your way. It's also easy to run away from your faith when you don't get your prayers and wishes granted.

I don't think its God's job to solve all our problems. Jesus isn't a magician or a genie. However, He is willing to help us take on the biggest life problem many of us will ever experience: the emptiness and loneliness that fills our hearts when we try to walk away from Him. Jesus is never startled by our life challenges. To the contrary, I'm convinced that He recognizes that our personal trials often serve to teach us just how much we need Him. Ultimately, we are given free will to decide whether we will follow the map He made for our lives or the map we want to draw for ourselves.

I believed I was entitled to the perfect *Janville* marriage and family. However, even if God had granted my wish, I couldn't have lived in perfect *Janville* because I'm not perfect. At the same time, I was unwilling to turn to Jesus and to trust in the plans He had for me. I wanted what I wanted, but God wanted something else for me—He wanted to teach me patience, perseverance, Christian character, and hope. I expected God to heal the emotional pain and separation I suffered as a result of my marriage failures. However, I was neither willing to request nor accept His healing for the spiritual emptiness I created each time I tried to run away from Him.

> Consider it pure joy . . . whenever you face trials of many kinds, because you know that the testing of your faith produces perseverance. Let perseverance finish its work so that you may be mature and complete, not lacking in anything.
> —James 1:2–4 NIV

> We also glory in our sufferings because, we know that suffering produces perseverance; perseverance character; and character, hope.
> —Romans 5:3–4 NIV

We all have choices to make when we get hit in the gut by life. We can isolate ourselves in resentment or we can try, with the help of Jesus, to choose the path of joy, peace, and reconciliation. Despite my generally optimistic view of life, I was trending toward bitterness and anger when Jesus sent the hail to knock some sense into me.

Looking backward, it became clear that while I had been praying for years for Jesus to transform Bill, I hadn't been praying for Him to transform me. When my prayers weren't answered as I demanded, I wanted a divorce from Bill (and from God). Not only was I not abiding in Jesus;

I actually thought for a period of time that I needed to cut myself off from Him if he wouldn't listen to me.

> "I am the vine; you are the branches. If you remain in me and I in you, you will bear much fruit; apart from me you can do nothing. If you do not remain in me, you are like a branch that is thrown away and withers . . . If you remain in me and my words remain in you, ask whatever you wish, and it will be done for you."
> —John 15:5–8 NIV

I had become strangely familiar and comfortable with my *Janland* pattern of worry and anxiety over my marital issues, even as I demanded that God bless the *Janplans* I thought would solve my problems. I didn't trust Him enough to ask Him to show me His plans for addressing my problems.

Even though I remained a believer, I had really shoved God in a box. I didn't believe He could help me—or that He wanted to help me. I made Him tiny and small. I didn't allow Him to be the omnipotent, omniscient, omnipresent, almighty God of the universe . . . the God who is far, far, far bigger than any of my little problems.

> Many are the plans in a person's heart, but it is the Lord's purpose that prevails.
> —Proverbs 19:21 NIV

> And we know that in all things God works for the good of those who love him, who have been called according to his purpose.
> —Romans 8:28 NIV

> "Do not worry about your life, what you will eat or drink; or about your body, what you will wear. Is not

> life more than food, and the body more than clothes?
> . . . **But s**eek first his kingdom and his righteousness,
> and all these things will be given to you as well. There-
> fore do not worry about tomorrow, for tomorrow will
> worry about itself."
> —Matthew 6:25, 33–34 NIV

Almost as rapidly as the storm that passed that afternoon, I suddenly began to believe that Jesus had a plan for me. All I needed to do
was open my heart and mind to seek His will, not my own. To give Him
control, to finally submit and let Him lead.

What was His plan? While I wasn't certain where God wanted to
use my gifts, I had discovered over time that Jesus made me to be a
people person. He gave me the gifts of compassion, empathy, humor,
and communication with other people.

Over the next several days, as I prayed about things, I begin to believe that Jesus wanted me to use the person-to-person skills He gave
me to reach out to others. Not as Jan, the codependent facilitator who
worked to solve problems partially so people would like her. No, I
needed to be transformed. I needed to become Jan, the healthy, Christ-
centered servant who would let God direct her giving. In fact, over the
course of a couple of weeks, it began to dawn on me that my twisted
life story might even be helpful to others who have experienced abuse
in marriage, control issues, and lack of faith.

At last, my mind and heart were open and receptive to His teaching.
I felt He was talking to me in plain language I could finally understand.
It was clear to me now . . . no more *Janplan*s . . . no more hiding from
God . . . no more prayers telling Christ what to do. And no more fears of
divine retribution for the errors of my past.

> For all have sinned and fallen short of the glory of God,
> and all are justified freely by his grace through the re-
> demption that came by Christ Jesus.
> —Romans 3:23–24 NIV

"All things are possible with God."
—Mark 10:27 NIV

I was beginning to see that my lifelong belief that I needed to be tough and to solve all my problems was also the ultimate expression of personal pride and arrogance. I wanted to try harder, pray louder, and work my way up to God's acceptance and forgiveness. In reality, God didn't want my works. He didn't want me to try to build a ladder of achievements to claw my way into heaven. He had already come down to meet me in my brokenness. All he wanted was my contrite heart.

"My grace is sufficient for you, for my power is made perfect in weakness."
—2 Corinthians 12:9 NIV

For I desire mercy, not sacrifice, and acknowledgment of God rather than burnt offerings.
—Hosea 6:6 NIV

God's grace is freely given to all of us, even people like me who have made a life of trying to run away from their hurts, sins, and personal deficiencies. Suddenly, the truth of God's everlasting love and forgiveness seemed real to me. I knew that His truth was going to give me freedom from my past.

"If you hold to my teaching, you are really my disciples. Then you will know the truth, and the truth will set you free.
—John 8:31–32 NIV

"Therefore go and make disciples of all nations, baptizing them in the name of the Father and of the Son and

of the Holy Spirit, and teaching them to obey everything I have commanded you."
　　　　　　　—Matthew 28:19–20 NIV

Dismantling, Releasing, and Listening
Within days of my gardening epiphany, I phoned my oldest son, Mark,
and told him I was coming home. We both cried like babies during
the call. Mark had been one of only a few people who had voiced any
support for my UK move. He probably did so partially because he had
grown up during two of his parents' dysfunctional marriages. As my
oldest, he most clearly understood that Bill and I were not good for
each other.

A few days later, I was on a flight back to the United States. I stayed
with Mark and helped shuttle his son to school while I contemplated
the logistics of dismantling my brief life in the UK.

I had a house to sell in Dover. I was probably going to take a financial
bath on that purchase. I would need to contact friends and family to
explain my decision to return, including responding to their skeptical
reactions and questions. Also, I had sold my home in Woodland Hills
before leaving for England. I had nowhere to live when I returned to
the States. I would have no job or any source of income once I arrived.
Regardless, I knew I needed to find a church home as soon as possible.

In July 2015, I listed my Dover home for sale and started packing.
Fortunately, I found a buyer for the house relatively quickly and at a
price that was a healthy percentage of what I originally paid. Neighbors
Kera and Mac were a great help to me as I prepared to leave England. I
was so thankful for their friendship.

I also immersed myself in prayer and in quiet meditation. The nature of my prayers now changed radically from the strident pleading
I sent heavenward in years past. Instead of instructions and demands
that my life circumstances fit my *Janville* dreams, I was now offering
thanks and praise to Jesus for His love, His grace, and His blessings. I
was also working to quiet my mouth and my brain in order that I might

pay attention to His voice. Enough of Jan the talker . . . time for Jan to become the listener.

> He says, "Be still, and know that I am God."
> —Psalm 46:10 NIV

> Do not worship any other god, for the Lord, whose name is Jealous, is a jealous God.
> —Exodus 34:14 NIV

> Seek his will in all you do, and he will show you which path to take.
> —Proverbs 3:6 NLT

Children, Grandchildren, and Unconditional Love

During the hailstorm in England, part of my awakening entailed the recognition that my kids and my grandkids mean everything to me. Of course, my *Janville* dream had been all about having that close, loving, *Leave It to Beaver* family that I never had growing up. I had devoted my life to trying to mold Bill into the loving husband and spiritual leader that would direct my *Janville* family. It didn't happen, but I refused to walk away from the dream. Given my lifelong desire for a happy, stable Christian family, how could I have ever believed that moving away from my family across the Atlantic Ocean was a good idea?

I was learning the hard way that when we immerse ourselves in self-pity, strange things happen. Our decisions become almost totally self-centered. It is easy to very quickly lose perspective on what is really of value in our lives. We play the blame game; we make *Janplans*.

Our exclusive focus becomes what we think we need in order to make ourselves "happy"—and our happiness is usually defined as the temporary emotions we feel in any given moment. To feel better, we often turn to worldly things, like the accumulation of material stuff, power, status, and a host of other small-*g* gods that we think will fill our empty cup. Not surprisingly, my anger and my self-centeredness led me to a very dark place as I focused on Jan's "happiness" and planned my escape to the UK—a place where I would be far removed from the light of God's presence.

> For you were once darkness, but now you are light in the Lord. Live as children of light (for the fruit of the light consists in all goodness, righteousness and truth) and find out what pleases the Lord.
> —Ephesians 5:8–10 NIV

> Do not store up for yourselves treasures on earth, where moths and vermin destroy, and where thieves break in and steal. But store up for yourselves treasures in heaven . . . For where your treasure is, there your heart will be also.
> —Matthew 6:19–21 NIV

When the hail pelted me in England, it startled me into recognizing that I had to be the person God created me to be, not the person I thought would make me happy. I am a people person and a mother. I need my relationships with my family and friends to feel whole. I had to recognize that it didn't matter if my family could never really live in my *Janville* dream with me. We still needed to be a family; one bound together with love, regardless of our personal imperfections or difficult family dynamics.

I also knew I had a responsibility to model how a Christian mother and grandmother should act, even if Bill and I failed to model how Christian parents should act. I needed to show my kids and grandkids, by my actions and behaviors, not just my words, that my I am a true follower of Christ and that my life has been richly blessed as a result.

The righteous lead blameless lives; blessed are their
children after them.
—Proverbs 20:7 NIV

Direct your children onto the right path, and when
they are older, they will not leave it.
—Proverbs 22:6 NLT

Returning to Jesus on the Return Home
In August 2015, as I sat in my seat on British Airways on the trip back
to Los Angeles, I had a tremendous sense of relief and peace. Despite
all the unanswered, practical questions about where and how I would
live once I returned, I wasn't worried. I knew I could trust God. I was
certain He would take care of me.

Keep your lives free from the love of money and be
content with what you have, because God has said,
"Never will I leave you; never will I forsake you."
—Hebrews 13:5 NIV

"So don't worry about tomorrow, for tomorrow will
bring its own worries. Today's trouble is enough for
today."
—Matthew 6:34 NLT

My last divorce from Bill was finalized in May 2015. I felt some sadness as I reflected on the difficult years we spent together. However, for
the first time, I was not feeling guilty. I was certain that the Lord's plans
for me were good. He had a plan to help me recover my emotional and
spiritual health. He had a plan for me to work to help build His kingdom. And I was confident that His plans did not involve an off-and-on-
again dysfunctional, angry relationship with Bill.

> "For I know the plans I have for you," declares the
> Lord, "plans to prosper you and not to harm you, plans
> to give you hope and a future."
> —Jeremiah 29:11 NIV

I could see now that, for decades, I misunderstood the concepts of forgiveness and reconciliation. In my relationships with Bill, I had always believed that if I was going to follow the biblical teaching of forgiveness, I also needed to reconcile and return to our marriage. On the way home from England, I finally understood that, while I needed to forgive from the depths of my heart, God was not commanding me to return to an abusive marriage. Forgiveness did not mean I was somehow also required to forget the hurts I had incurred during our three marriages. As the long flight headed toward the West Coast, I prayed sincerely for a soft, benevolent heart.

Staring at the puffy clouds on the flight back, I wasn't feeling any anger toward Bill. I wasn't even upset about his recent admission, offered after our third divorce became final, that he never, ever stopped drinking, despite his repetitive promises to the contrary. I finally got it . . . I couldn't make him stop. That was his decision. God hadn't given me the power or authority to fix anyone.

> Do not repay anyone evil for evil. Be careful to do what
> is right in the eyes of everyone. If it is possible, as far as
> it depends on you, live at peace with everyone.
> —Romans 12:17–18 NIV

> "Do not judge, and you will not be judged. Do not condemn, and you will not be condemned. Forgive, and
> you will be forgiven."
> —Luke 6:37 NIV

Upon my return, I quickly reconnected with my family and friends. Tears were shed as I tried to express to each of them how much I missed them and how glad I was to be home. Everyone was very kind. I think they all understood that I recognized my mistakes, that I was yearning to restart our relationships and to make amends for any hurt I had caused.

As human beings, we can't fully comprehend how the Lord works. However, He understands our needs and, oftentimes, His responses to some of our needs are nothing short of miraculous. I was finally willing to trust that I could put my life in Christ's hands. After all, He made me. I knew His plans had to be far better than the ones I had been making.

> "For my thoughts are not your thoughts, neither are your ways my ways," declares the LORD. "As the heavens are higher than the earth, so are my ways higher than your ways and my thoughts than your thoughts."
> —Isaiah 55:8–9 NIV

> If God is for us, who can be against us? He who did not spare his own Son, but gave him up for us all—how will he not also, along with him, graciously give us all things?
> —Romans 8:31–32 NIV

I understood that I was broken. What I didn't fully understand yet was that, through His grace, Jesus would literally shower this prodigal daughter with gifts upon her return. Of course, I didn't deserve His favor after *Janplan: Europa*. Still, despite my rebelliousness, He was there for me. Here are just a few examples of how God provided me with exactly what I needed, when I needed it, once I came back to Him and back to California.

Shelter for the Body and the Soul

Mark and his family kindly offered me a temporary place to stay as I searched Craigslist for housing after returning to the LA area. One of the first people I met in my search was Rachel, a homeowner who was renting out a room in her house after recently losing her husband to heart failure. Her rental unit didn't work out for me, but Rachel and I hit it off after discovering we were both Christians. She even invited me to attend her Bible study group. Through her, I met an outstanding group of Christian women who encouraged me to dig into the Bible with them and who also helped me build up the frequency, sincerity, and depth of my prayer life.

A few days after meeting Rachel, I was offered a temporary room in a home that was being renovated prior to resale. The home didn't even have hot water during my stay. However, it provided me with a roof over my head at no cost while I searched for alternate housing. Further, the evening hours spent alone in my tiny room, furnished with an air mattress, small refrigerator, and forty-watt reading lamp, provided me with valuable devotional time. I spent my evenings reading the Bible, giving thanks for my blessings, and reflecting upon my growing relationship with the Lord.

Even with so little, I felt I had so much. My soul was finally at peace. I was so thankful for His presence. Jesus was using my time in this spartan room to teach me gratitude. I began to understand that I really didn't need many of the material things I had previously clung to and believed were absolutely critical to my wellbeing and my happiness.

At this point, I didn't have a home, furniture, a closet filled with clothing, or any of the other physical comforts that were formerly part of my life. However, I was beginning to grasp the reality that life really isn't about stuff; a new outfit, a new couch, and any other material comforts do not fill spiritual and emotional needs. Upon my return, I had my family, my friends, and my renewed relationship with Christ . . . all the essentials I really needed for a joyful life.

> "Therefore, I tell you, do not worry about your life, what you will eat; or about your body, what you will wear. Is not life more than food, and the body more than clothes. . . . "Consider how the wild flowers grow.

They do not labor or spin. Yet I tell you, not even Solomon in all his splendor was dressed like one of these."
—Luke 12:22–23, 27 NIV

"Let anyone who is thirsty come to me and drink. Whoever believes in me, as Scripture has said, rivers of living water will flow from within them."
—John 7:37–38 NIV

Katie and Stan: Christian Community and Service

Within a few days after my plane touched down in Southern California, God offered this lost sheep another gift. I joined a local gym near my rented room, and, after a Zumba workout, I started up a conversation with Katie, the woman next to me in the class. I soon learned that she was both an RN and a Christian pastor. She was teaching nursing classes and caring for her husband, Stan, who had been diagnosed with early onset Alzheimer's disease and for her sister who had cancer, while simultaneously leading her church community. I instantly felt compassion for this courageous woman while also recognizing that my life challenges paled in comparison to hers.

Katie and I quickly became good friends. I helped her church distribute clothing to the homeless in downtown Los Angeles the first weekend after we met at the gym. Later, I started periodically reading to her husband, Stan, who had already lost that ability as well as the mobility to move around the house without assistance. A short while later, after Katie fell down some stairs and fractured vertebrae in her neck and back, this girl, who needed to be needed, was needed.

I reached out to help Katie periodically by running errands, helping care for Stan, gardening, and handling other household needs. I was also certain that Jesus had placed me in this special relationship: one modeled on the type of sacrificial love and service that Christ demonstrated for His followers.

> "Just as the Son of Man did not come to be served, but
> to serve, and to give his life as a ransom for many."
> —Matthew 20:28 NIV

> "Truly I tell you, whatever you did for one of the least
> of these brothers and sisters of mine, you did for me."
> —Matthew 25:40 NIV

Returning to Church: A "Get To" Not a "Got To" Activity
My plane from England arrived in Los Angeles on a Thursday and I attended church in an LA suburb that Sunday. Getting to church this time wasn't a "*got to do it*," it was a "*get to do it*." It felt so good to sing hymns and praise songs. I really wanted to be in community with other believers and with Jesus. I wasn't there because I was forcing someone else to attend as punishment for bad behavior. I truly felt the Holy Spirit's presence embracing me and welcoming me back.

> For those who are led by the Spirit of God are the children of God.
> —Romans 8:14 NIV

After the service, I introduced myself to the senior pastor. I shed some tears as I explained that I had just returned from a few months in Europe—a trip motivated by my selfish desire to separate from my loved ones and to walk away from God. I acknowledged that many of the practical details of my future seemed uncertain at this point. But I told the pastor that I felt certain that the Lord would direct me, if I would just get out of the way and allow Him to lead.

The senior pastor was extremely comforting. He assured me that I was doing the right thing to return to my family, my friends, and Jesus. The pastor grabbed my hand and prayed with me. I instantly felt another touch from the Spirit, including a sense of renewed confidence that everything would work out according to God's planning and His timing.

He has made everything beautiful in its time.
—Ecclesiastes 3:11 NIV

And we know that in all things God works for the good of those who love him, who have been called according to his purpose.
—Romans 8:28 NIV

God's Voice in a Moment of Confusion

Unfortunately, a couple of weeks after I arrived back in LA, the codependent part of Jan began to prod me to call Bill. Somehow, I felt I needed to try to make amends for the anger both of us had felt as our third divorce was completed. In my mind, I needed to try to fix things one more time. Perhaps we could have peace within the family and also be at peace with the finality of our breakup.

Just as I was about to dial Bill's number, the Holy Spirit connection between my heart and my brain was raising a yellow flag. Feeling just a bit uncertain about the call, I decided I should first call my friend, Sarah Galano. Sarah and Dave Galano have been two of my closest friends since the time Bill and I first began seeing each other. They were part of the Hernandez group. They attended Village Bible Church with us. Dave and Bill occasionally fished and hunted together, and Sarah and I relied upon each other as we raised our kids. On occasion, I had also turned to the Galanos for counsel when experiencing family challenges through the years.

As I started to dial Sarah's cell, however, it dawned on me that my call would be an exercise in futility. Sarah *never* answers her cell directly. Every call goes into voicemail. However, on this day, to my amazement, just as I was about to hang up and call Bill, my friend picked up.

Sarah *screamed* at me when I disclosed the purpose of my call. "*NO, NO, NO,*" she literally yelled over the phone. Do not call Bill. Do not do anything that might send mixed signals. Do not offer a bumbling explanation that might be misinterpreted as an overture to reunite for a fourth time.

Instead, Sarah told me to pray, read the Bible, go to church, go to counseling, and turn to my friends and family. "Get strong, get with Jesus and get healthy, Jan," Sarah admonished.

I was shocked. Sarah never yells and she doesn't normally dictate to people. However, after working through things with her on the phone, I realized she was right. Jan was again trying to fix the unfixable. Jan was again feeling guilt over her decisions. The codependent Jan that wanted everyone to like her and accept her had resurfaced again.

I didn't call Bill. However, I did pray for him, and for me . . . for forgiveness and for a release of any anger that might interfere with our relationships with our kids. I also offered prayers of thanksgiving: prayers praising God for using Sarah as his mouthpiece to provide me with words of wisdom, just at the right time, to help me continue to heal and grow.

Children's Hospital: God's Healing Touch

After returning to the West Coast, God offered me another huge transformational insight. Jan, the people pleaser and everyone's problem solver, really needed to get over herself.

Too frequently, even while attending to others, it was really all about me. *Janville* was all about Jan . . . my dream, my needs, my perfect family, my happiness. Now God was prodding me to grasp a critical truth: it's not about me. I could only really follow *Him* if I was willing to walk away from *me*. To be a true follower of Jesus, I needed to focus on His agenda and priorities, not mine. If I was willing to walk away from my *Janplans,* I believed that Christ would point me to a purpose that was so much more significant and fulfilling than the worldly stuff I always believed would please Jan in the moment.

Wow . . . huge news flash . . . could it be that learning to love and accept myself actually meant getting over myself? It was time for me to accept God's grace, to walk away from my pity party and from my incessant desire to control the world around me. The "new Jan" needed to reach out to others, not for the payback they might give me, but solely for the love I could give them. This realization was a "wow" and an "ouch" all in the same moment.

After more prayer, I felt prompted to volunteer at Children's Hospital Los Angeles. The application process, just to become a volunteer, was far more rigorous than any job or college application I had ever completed. I wasn't even sure I had the emotional strength to handle being around really sick children.

Still, I felt God was pushing me to move beyond myself . . . to use my gifts of empathy, communication, and humor to touch some kids who were battling real life-and-death challenges. I sensed that these kids (and Jan) needed God's healing touch.

For three years, every Tuesday evening, I spent time at Children's Hospital playing games, doing crafts, reading, singing, and laughing with kids who had every reason to be bitter and sad about their lot in life. Inevitably, these kids brought me far more joy than I probably ever brought them. Now, as I lie in bed at night praying for each of them, I have a much deeper sense of gratitude for the blessings I have received in my life.

> "I showed you that by this kind of hard work we must help the weak, remembering the words the Lord Jesus himself said: 'It is more blessed to give than to receive.'"
> —Acts 20:35 NIV

> "Let your light shine before others, that they may see your good deeds and glorify your Father in heaven."
> —Matthew 5:16 NIV

God's Next Miracle: Providing My Christian Partner

Of course, my *Janville* dream, consisting of the perfect mate, perfect loving family, and perfect life, was unrealistic and unattainable. Since I am imperfect, how could I ever have expected a perfect life? Shedding my *PollyJana* dreams has helped me come to accept my own imperfections and those of the world in which I live.

At the same time, as I worked to alter my life perspective, I pondered whether my ongoing desire for a Christian partner was also completely unrealistic. Despite my myriad of mistakes, was this a prayer that God might grant? If I could just get out of the way and let Christ lead me, could I possibly find a man who would be devoted to both Jesus and me?

After my return from the UK, I started to ask these questions, always near the end of my prayers. After giving thanks for the wonderful blessings God showered into my life, I started to pray, "If it is your will, Father, I would love a Christian partner with whom I could share my life." For once, I wasn't demanding, ordering, or attempting to control. I wasn't trying to dictate the agenda, the timing, and the result. I wasn't trying to barter with God. I wasn't trying to cash in by claiming that the asset side of the self-created Jan ledger sheet was now sufficiently stacked such that my prayer should be granted. No, this time Jan's prayers were offered with a contrite heart.

> "Ask and it will be given to you; seek and you will find;
> knock and the door will be opened to you."
> —Matthew 7:7 NIV

After a few weeks of my repeated partnership prayers, I felt a nudge. *If you are looking for a Christian partner, look where Christian men can be found.* Ok, I thought . . . at church and . . .?

I really didn't have a clue where to look. When a good friend suggested a website called Christian Mingle, I decided to check it out, though I had never been on a dating website before.

I hopped on one evening, posted a couple of photos, and wrote a three-sentence profile entitled, "Searching for a Christian Partner." I simply noted that I was a follower of Jesus and that I highly valued my family and my friends. I was interested in meeting someone who might become a Christian partner and who would allow me to be me.

I received a flood of responses. However, after meeting a few men for coffee, by late September 2015, I decided that it probably wasn't God's timing for me. Above all, I knew that I needed to be patient. I had to let Jesus lead. My *Janplans* had consistently led to hurried, controlling, non-Christ centered, dysfunctional relationships. Not this time . . .

The day before I was going to place my three-month Christian Mingle membership on inactive status, I did a final search to see who had checked out my profile. In doing so, I ran across the photo of a guy whose profile said he was primarily interested in meeting a Christian woman just for friendship.

I was attracted to his photo and his profile. Interestingly enough, on the surface, he was just what Bill always said I would be looking for: a handsome, successful attorney. However, that wasn't the part of his profile that caught my attention. Rather, it was his statement that he had a life dream that paralleled mine: being part of a real and growing Christian partnership.

Great. However, I had a big problem. This guy had apparently looked briefly at my profile and photos and then . . . moved on. I was instantly curious why he hadn't sent me at least a wink or a short note like most of the other men had done. So, I did a *JanThing*. I wrote him and asked why he had looked but decided not to contact me. He wrote back with a couple of questions.

New to the LA area, he said he was just looking for some Christian friends. He indicated that he didn't recognize the name of my town, noting that he wasn't interested in a "long drive" to make a new friend. He was also curious about whether I "looked like my photos," observing that he had met a couple other women who apparently didn't make any effort to attach current photos to their profiles.

Somewhat miffed, I almost didn't respond. When I did, I commented that I felt like I was being interviewed for a job. I urged him to Google my location, if he had the energy and aptitude, and yes, my photos were current—what about his? Apparently, my sense of humor appealed to him. I received a compliment and an apology for his rather terse initial response. After exchanging a few emails in which we both emphasized the importance of pursuing our Christian walk, we decided to get together for a pizza.

I almost cancelled our meeting. Given my previously unsuccessful contacts on this dating service, I wondered if God was sending me a prompting that it wasn't His timing for me to move forward. I was fine with that result, but I waited a bit too long to cancel the pizza date and then felt obligated to at least show up at the appointed time and location.

Truthfully, I wasn't in a great mood that day. I wasn't about to patronize this guy if he didn't like the real Jan, live and in-person. I arrived early and didn't even go into the restaurant. I decided I would meet him in the parking lot, and I would make it a very short meeting if there didn't appear to be mutual interest. As he was getting out of his car in the parking lot, I walked up, stuck out my hand, quickly introduced myself and said, "So this is what you get. Do I look like my photos?" He flashed an embarrassed smile and faked a retreat to his car before we shared a good laugh. The ice was broken.

The pizza was good, but the company was better. Greg was tall, handsome, smart, and funny. Most importantly, it was clear from the outset that he loved God. He had given up a successful career as an attorney in the Midwest to move to California to work with an environmental nonprofit because he was passionate about the pressing need to halt climate change. He has two grown boys that he loves very much, both of whom are married with families. He doesn't care about money or status, but he does care about serving the homeless and others who are less fortunate. He is an amazing listener, strong in his spiritual convictions, but calm in his demeanor.

From the inception of our first meeting, Greg and I both worked very hard at establishing two core concerns as we did the "getting to know you" thing. First, neither of us were interested in spending time with someone who wasn't genuinely sincere about sharing their walk with Christ. Secondly, neither of us were interested in being with someone who wouldn't accept us just as we are . . . with all of our imperfections, deficiencies, and any other "baggage." For once, I didn't feel like

I was being judged or that Greg was someone who might be more interested in controlling me than just loving me.

By the end of our second meeting, both of us had fully disclosed our checkered marital histories. Greg is no saint. He's not the hero of my story. He is a man who has made plenty of mistakes in his life. In fact, his story of past marital failures is also shaped by acts of selfishness and shallow faith. Because of our willfulness, both of us have experienced periods of estrangement from God and from our families—separations that taught each of us valuable but painful lessons about faith and love. As a result, both of us were far more willing to walk away from this connection than to walk into another failed relationship.

Within a few weeks, it was clear to each of us that God was in the middle of this friendship. We attended church together, read daily devotionals, prayed together, served together, confided in each other, had fun together, laughed and even cried together. The miracle that we both had prayed for through the years appeared to be happening . . . God was blessing each of us with an opportunity to have a Christian partner He had chosen for us.

For my part, I felt I had finally met a man who would be trustworthy, devoted to God and to our relationship, and who would accept me as I am. For Greg, I believe I represented someone who really wanted to grow in her relationship with the Lord, who didn't care at all about his bank account balance, who had a sense of humor, and who might become his best friend and partner.

Early in our relationship, we adopted a motto to serve as the guiding light for our developing friendship: "God First, Us Second, the Rest is Detail." Both of us have grappled with low self-esteem—a by-product of emotional abuse. Both of us have made some extremely poor relationship and life decisions that have pulled us away from Jesus and our loved ones. As a consequence, we both understood, without reservation, that if we failed to put God first, we were likely destined to repeat the mistakes and heartaches of the past.

As our relationship developed, I think it became apparent to both of us that I could also benefit from some professional counseling assistance as I begin to establish a new and very different life, away from the chaos and abuse I experienced with Bill. Greg gently guided me toward that step. A short time later, through a referral from my new church home, I began meeting with Patty, an excellent Christian counselor.

Patty had both personal and professional expertise in dealing with codependency, substance abuse, addictive behaviors, and family dysfunction. Over the course of several months, her incredibly insightful way of communicating Christian and psychological wisdom moved me from expressions of self-pity and anger to feelings of self-acceptance, confidence, faith, and hope.

Patty didn't pull any punches during our sessions. While being sensitive to my emotional fragility, Patty didn't coddle me with fifty minutes of "So how did that make you feel?" questions each session. Patty thoroughly understood the underlying causes of addiction and codependency, as well as the triggers, cycles, and rationalizations that people use to justify their feelings and behaviors.

When I would start the process of "coulda, woulda, shoulda," chiding myself for not being able to "fix" my ex and our marriages, she would often stop me and simply ask, "So, Jan, tell me what your Monday would look like if you were still in the marriage? How about your Tuesday?" and so on. By forcing me to look realistically at my daily life, including my ongoing fears, uncertainties, frustrations, and disappointments, Patty helped me see that I still had a tendency to glorify a relationship that never really existed. Most importantly, she helped me understand that I was not God and that I should not try to play Him in my life relationships.

Over several months of sessions, I gradually felt myself growing stronger. With Jesus as my new anchor, I was learning to move away from looking at life exclusively from Jan's perspective and to look at things more from Jesus's perspective. Forgiveness, love, grace, and compassion were starting to fill in the emptiness in my heart that anger, self-pity, and the desire to control others had created.

Patty's considerate but strong guidance has also helped me understand that Bill's perpetual intimidation had actually rewired my brain, training me to try to avoid conflict at all costs. Patty gently but firmly led me to embrace the freedom offered by improved mental, emotional, and spiritual health. For the first time in my life, I felt I could actually walk away from the more familiar but dysfunctional prison that confined me to reactions based on frustration, fear, and codependent behaviors.

My husband, Greg, remained my cheerleader during the long months of my chaos withdrawal. We were married by my friend Katie a year after we met. Greg calmly offered me love, emotional support, and a patient ear as I worked through my issues. He has also been my spiritual accountability partner. I needed help as I weaned myself off the adrenaline-fueled addiction to chaos and spiritual darkness in which I had been immersed. Through each step in the process, he has helped both of us keep our eye on our "true north." Jesus must come first. Our relationship is second, and we acknowledge, often with a smile, that the rest of life is really just about "detail."

Bill's Gone: What Is the Cost of "Freedom"?

A couple of years after my return to the States, Bill took his own life. He ended his life the same way he lived it . . . on his own terms. Over time, Bill had developed congestive heart failure, partially due to a sedentary lifestyle he adopted after he fell on some ice and was injured. Before his passing, Bill regularly expressed frustration that the people around him were not as helpful as he thought they should be and that his deteriorating health prevented him from having the freedom to pursue his love of fishing.

Shortly before his death, his cardiologist had encouraged Bill to improve his health with diet and exercise. His last meal of a pizza, a chocolate cake, and a few beers apparently signaled what he thought of his doctor's advice.

As I came to grips with his action, my first thoughts were of concern for my boys. Each would be grieving in his own way, but I wanted to be there for them. The experience was hard on my sons, but they are strong men. They understood what their dad valued in life. They recognized both his many good and bad personal qualities.

I experienced a broad cadre of emotions. I felt sadness for Bill's decision, for the torment he was obviously feeling at the time, and for the impact his action would have on the people who loved him. I felt grief that the prayers I offered for his recovery and general well-being were not to be answered before his death. I felt disappointment that Bill was never able to move beyond his anger toward me to act in the best interests of our kids and grandkids. I experienced remorse that I spent the majority of my life trying to fix a relationship that could not be fixed.

Several months after his death, however, I started to feel a new joy. I was able to embrace a growing sense of freedom from my past; freedom from my largely self-imposed guilt and from our family legacy of emotional abuse. I also felt freedom from the controlling presence Bill had continued to impose on our family, even long after our final divorce.

Let me be candid. I also experienced some validation after Bill's passing. Of course, I didn't rejoice or revel in the fact that he was gone. I had forgiven Bill for his mistakes in our marriages. I knew the great qualities Bill had and I recognized the potential he had to be a terrific man, husband, and father. I certainly did not feel any joy over his death. Still, as a confused codependent for most of my life, I had always believed it was my duty to solve the "Bill problem" and to make him happy. I felt validation that I finally understood that it was okay to accept the reality that Bill was not my "fix-it" project, nor was I responsible for his behavior.

My Transformed, Personal Relationship with Jesus

So, what is my life like now, nearly six years after I finally embraced Christ's grace and love after the hailstorm in the UK?

I finally get that Jesus loves me unconditionally. It doesn't matter whether I'm having a bad hair day or if the roast got cold before the potatoes were done. He isn't interested in a perfect, Martha Stewart woman of the house. He doesn't want a BFF or a relationship that is contingent on my efforts to curry His friendship, to amass good works, or to display evidence of worldly success.

The Christ I follow is the omnipotent, omniscient, omnipresent, all-powerful God and Master of the universe. Yet He still cares about me as I live out my life as a very imperfect human being. He listens to me. He forgives me. He loves me without reservation. I am one of His children.

Jesus sacrificed His life for me to defeat my sin and my death. He offers His loving grace to me, regardless of the number of times I have stumbled and failed to follow His plan for my life. He is infinitely patient with me. He is steadfast and unchanging. He offers the truth that has set me free from a self-constructed jail cell walled in by fear, remorse, self-loathing, and guilt . . . a cell that kept me chained up for decades.

What on this earth could surpass the unconditional love of this kind of relationship?

I reaped a good deal of heartache and disappointment before I came to understand that chasing an unrealistic dream, pursuing material things, and constantly seeking the approval of others could never fill the emptiness I felt in my life. Only a personal relationship with Jesus Christ could provide me with the love, security, and stability that I believed only existed in *Janville*.

> Do not conform to the pattern of this world, but be transformed by the renewing of your mind. Then you will be able to test and approve what God's will is—his good, pleasing and perfect will.
> —Romans 12:2 NIV

> "Yes, I am the vine; you are the branches. Those who remain in me, and I in them, will produce much fruit. For apart from me you can do nothing. Anyone who does not remain in me is thrown away like a useless branch and withers. Such branches are gathered into a pile to be burned. But if you remain in me and my

words remain in you, you may ask for anything you want, and it will be granted!"
—John 15:5–7 NLT

And I am convinced that nothing can ever separate us from God's love. Neither death nor life, neither angels nor demons, neither our fears for today nor our worries about tomorrow—not even the powers of hell can separate us from God's love.
—Romans 8:38 NLT

No *PollyJana, Janville, or Janplans*: Living a Real Life with Jesus
Is it easy to live my new life as a committed follower of Jesus?

Not always. I still wrestle with my humanness including my uncertainty, frustration, fear, mistrust, and low self-confidence. As a codependent, I still battle my engrained propensity to want to fix others and their problems. As a resident of this world, I still struggle with the woman who so earnestly wanted to be loved and accepted by everyone.

As I am learning to love myself, I can also see that Jan, the consummate people pleaser, spent much of her life trying to be a codependent God pleaser. I wanted God to like me. I was focused far more on accumulating good deeds to fill up the asset side of what I perceived to be God's "Judging Jan" ledger than I was on embracing Christ's promises of grace, love, and mercy. As a result, many of my important life decisions were motivated by a desire to curry God's favor and avoid His punishment rather than by a desire to accept and display His love and His grace in the way I lived my life.

I have also learned that, when your brain has been wired to constantly react to uncertainty and disruption, it can be a challenge to rewire it—to learn to live without the daily drama. In fact, adjusting to a new normal—that is, a stable, non-reactive life—can even seem boring at times because your system is not receiving its anticipated regular jolt of trauma and crisis. I have even experienced a real physical withdrawal from the constant anxiety I felt in my former life.

As a recovering victim of emotional abuse, I have also experienced some grief on the way to appreciating my new normal. Most of us find some degree of comfort in what we know, even if it is unhealthy for us. Change is always hard. However, the only constant in life is change. Changing one's thinking patterns, reactions, behaviors, and outlook on life can be extremely difficult. During the process of change, many doubts (including those planted by the Evil One) will try to bump us off the road to spiritual and emotional health.

For me, struggling with changes in my relationships with my adult boys has been my primary source of doubt. As expected, Bill reacted with anger following our final split. He tried to build alliances with the kids and grandkids to exclude me. My family life, though on the road to its own new normal, was not the same.

As a result, as I continue to walk my path to recovery, I can still find myself wondering what I might have done differently to protect my relationships with my family. Yet, even as I navigate change and some grief associated with my loss of the familiar, I have never seriously questioned my decision to choose this new path—the one leading to Jesus, pursuing the truth and freedom He provides; the path that offers spiritual, mental, and emotional health; the life path that is right for me.

I used to think of myself as a tough girl partially because I put up with so much dysfunction at home. Now I realize that I was actually a weak girl—one who ran away from God, her family, and the reality of her life. Rather than grabbing the hand of Jesus and relying upon my faith, prayer, and the support of my Christian community to help me fight through my trials, I always chose flight . . . the easy but temporary escape from difficulties.

Each time I ran away, however, I added baggage to the heavy sled of accumulated guilt, anger, and sadness that I was already pulling along from my past. It shouldn't have come as a surprise to me that, after only a few weeks in the UK, the weight of my unresolved sin and regret brought my sled, and my life, to a screeching, sudden stop.

I have shed my sled. Now, by accepting God's grace and forgiveness for my past, I'm free to live a joyful life, confronting life's challenges head-on with the help of Jesus. I'm also learning the discipline of discipleship as I try to live joyfully in the present, focusing on Christ one thought, one action, one day at a time.

Don't get me wrong: the Christian walk is not an easy one. We live in a material, prideful world that constantly beckons us to succumb to its glittery temptations, including the popular thinking that the rest of the world exists to make us happy. The path of walking away from yourself and toward Jesus is not always smooth. Learning to follow Christ takes discipline and a dedication to quit focusing solely on your personal desires, needs, and preferences.

I've also walked away from *PollyJana*, the naive dreamer with her lifelong fantasy of the perfect family. I know that it is a continuing process to learn to live as a Christian. I will never arrive at a place of full Christian maturity in my lifetime. However, now I feel that I can look forward, with excitement, to my life journey, including whatever trials and hardships may arise along the way, with assurance that Jesus is making the trip with me. I have said goodbye to the emotional abuse, chaos, disappointment, anger, and pain that captivated my life. I have been transformed by the presence of Jesus in my life. I now try to live one day at a time, feeling gratitude, peace, and overall contentment by being thankful for what Christ has done in my life.

I work daily to harness and discipline my thoughts and emotions so that I will trust God and live in the present. I am also working to demonstrate Christ-centered love, not only to my family and friends, but to the world of my neighbors. Rather than relying upon *Janplans*, I'm relying upon JesusPlans. Now I am blessed to embrace the life God created and planned for me. It is so much better than the artificial *Janville* life I tried to create and plan for myself.

My Simple Answer Can Be Your Simple Answer

Perhaps what has changed my life can change your life. No matter what challenges you face in your life—whether addiction, codependence, estrangement from family or friends, difficulty at work, financial stress, or any other problem—a real relationship with God can transform you and lead you to freedom. It doesn't matter what you have done or what has happened to you in the past—Jesus opens His arms to you. He will love you and accept you! Jesus can, and will, perform a miracle that will give you hope and a new life!

Like any real friendship, however, developing your relationship with Him requires a commitment on your part. You have to believe that Jesus, God's son, died to pardon your sins and your death. You need trust that He has a plan for your life—a plan that will gradually be revealed through your obedience to His commands and by your time spent reading the Bible, in prayer, in fellowship with other believers, and in service.

If you are at all like me, you will struggle with patience, including waiting on God for His answers. You will also be challenged to trust Him when He says no to your prayer requests. Still, I offer my written testimony, pulled from four decades of *Janplans* and the heartache, pain, and anxiety they caused, to affirm one simple truth: Jesus saves broken people. He works miracles. Here, now, today. I'm living proof. He can and He will transform your life, if you will reach out and grab His hand.

It feels great trusting God. It feels great submitting to His leadership and following His direction for our lives. It feels great letting Him control the world He made. He does a far better job at it than we can ever hope to do.

The Confession

I am not in control.

I cannot control all my people.

I cannot control the situation. Even when I want what is best, I cannot control the outcome.

I cannot make people behave. I cannot make people believe.

I cannot make people be strong. Because I am not God.

He alone knows the end from the beginning.

He alone knows how things will turn out.
I hereby fire myself from His job.
And I see my fight for control as what it really is,
A screaming testament to my distrust.
Lord, help me trust You more.

—Beth Moore

Printed in the United States
by Baker & Taylor Publisher Services